Explorations in Theology 4

Explorations in Theology 4

MAURICE WILES

SCM PRESS LTD

334 01974 5

First published 1979
by SCM Press Ltd
58 Bloomsbury Street, London WC1

Phototypeset in VIP Palatino by
Input Typesetting Ltd, London
Printed in Great Britain by
Richard Clay (The Chaucer Press) Ltd
Bungay, Suffolk

Contents

Preface

The three lectures that constitute the first part of this collection were given as the 1977 Kellogg Lectures at Episcopal Divinity School, Cambridge, Massachusetts. They are published here for the first time. I would like to take this opportunity of expressing my gratitude to the School for the honour of being invited to lecture on that Foundation. My wife and I received outstandingly generous hospitality from the whole community at the School throughout a stay of several weeks. A special word of thanks is due to Harvey Guthrie Jr who presided over all the arrangements for our visit with the same imperturbable kindness with which he oversees the life of the School, and to Don and Anne Winslow who prompted the visit in the first place and prepared us by the hospitality of their own home for the hospitality of the School itself.

The first of these three lectures also incorporates some material first used in the 1975 Maynard-Chapman Divinity Lecture at Westfield College, London, under the title 'Faith, Doubt and Theology'.

The fourth lecture, 'The Patristic Appeal to Tradition', is also newly published here. It was first given as a guest lecture at the Sacred Heart School of Theology, Hales Corner, Wisconsin, where I was again recipient of most generous hospitality.

The remaining papers have all appeared in print before and are reproduced here virtually without change. Details of their original publication are given in the notes at the end.

Introduction

Most theologians writing in England at the present time have an official position in the university rather than in the church. Though often ordained ministers of a church, it is the university which pays them and which provides the primary setting for their work. This undoubtedly has an effect on the issues to which they direct their attention and the style in which their work is done. But it is sometimes suggested that the effect is even more far-reaching, that it has given rise to theological developments which though appropriate to the setting of the university can only be of disservice to the life of the church. Yet if both university and church are concerned with truth, we can hardly allow that the dichotomy is as sharp as that.

The invitation to give the Kellogg lectures at Episcopal Divinity School, Cambridge, Massachusetts, was an invitation to lecture to alumni of the School now serving in the parochial ministry of the Episcopal Church and to students in preparation for that ministry. I had to ask myself whether the critical approach to theology which I was developing in my own studies was of relevance or value to such an audience. So I made it my aim in those lectures to present an approach to theology primarily developed in the context of university work, without any diminution of the critical rigour that is properly looked for there, and to present it as something of vital importance to the life of the church as a whole.

I have twice had to deliver an inaugural lecture as a university professor of theology.[1] The first lecture in this collection sets out to fulfil the same sort of task in relation to the role of critical theology in the church. The second and third lectures, which were designed to form an integrated series with it, go on to apply that method to two central issues of Christian belief. The lectures were written at about the same time as *The Myth of God*

Incarnate[2] and delivered shortly before its publication. The subjects discussed in the second and third lectures here – the impact
on christology of historical studies and of the study of other
religions – are the two issues that are central to the argument of
that book. These lectures enable me to set out my own position
in relation to them somewhat more fully. Since the lectures are
printed here very much in the form in which they were delivered with only minor modifications arising out of the discussions to which they gave rise at the time, they do not take into
account the later discussion to which *The Myth of God Incarnate*
has given rise.

One of the basic challenges that is often raised against this
critical style of theology as a form of theological activity within
the life of the church is that it runs counter to the church's sense
of being within a living tradition and also to the essentially historical character of Christian faith. The two papers that make up
the second part of this collection are concerned with that issue.
Thus although one is an examination of attitudes in the patristic
period and the other in the modern, they belong closely
together. The two papers seek to explore ways in which the
church has traditionally handled its own tradition and historically has understood its own historicity. Neither the church's
tradition nor the historical character of the faith are as straightforward concepts as might appear at first sight.

Thus Part II looks back to what may be seen as theoretical
difficulties about adopting a critical approach to theology at the
heart of the church's life. Part III looks forward to another area
where doubts and questions may reasonably be raised. Can
such an approach help us with such 'churchly' concerns of
theology as worship, ministry and sacraments? This is not an
area in which I have written much. I include these four papers as
some indication of the way in which it might be done. The first
was written at a much earlier date (1963) than any of the other
papers in this collection but it does express in very general terms
the way in which I would still want to approach many of the
questions that arise in this area of theology. The next two papers
are devoted to the Bible and the eucharist respectively. What
they have in common is the belief that in the past Christian
accounts of both have often been too narrow and too specific in
character. What I have tried to do in these two articles (which

were originally quite independent of one another and written
with no consciousness of any connection between them in my
mind) is to bring out the breadth of the significance of both
scripture and the eucharist for the life of the Christian community. I believe that this may prove to be an important approach to
our understanding of them in the future, in the light of the sort
of critical study reflected in the first two parts of this collection.
The final paper brings together my interest in patristic studies
and in the ecumenical concerns of the church today. It does so in
a way which, I hope, shows the value of reflecting on such
contemporary concerns in the light of the past practice of the
church, without succumbing to the mistake (which I have often
criticized in others) of trying to determine present practice by
past precedent.

1

The Role of a Critical Theology in the Church Today

Oxford is traditionally the home of lost causes, the city of dreaming spires where the practice of an ancient piety can continue undisturbed by changes in the surrounding world. If that is the traditional picture, I can only say that it doesn't feel like that – not all the time anyway. The intellectual and practical changes of our time impinge even upon an Oxford theologian. And such changes always pose a grave dilemma for the theologian – indeed for the church as a whole. If in intended loyalty to the faith once for all delivered to the saints one resists all change, the likely outcome is to confine the gospel that is meant for the market-place to an intellectual ghetto and in the name of truth to turn one's back on truth. If on the other hand one seeks to adapt the gospel to every wind of intellectual change, one runs the risk of presenting as Christian gospel the latest ideas of the psychologist and the sociologist at the very moment when their originators are discarding them as outworn theories. Somewhere between those two extremes there lies a path that the theologian must help the church to find. The way forward is never clear or simple, and there are bound to be serious tensions and disagreements as differing proposals are made about where it lies. One man's fidelity to tradition is another man's obscurantism; one man's contemporary interpretation of the faith is another man's selling of the pass.

In this first lecture I want to try to define more precisely the nature of the critical theologian's task, and in the two lectures that follow I shall try to fulfil that role in relation to two central areas of Christian belief. Whether or not you agree in the end with the path that I suggest, I hope you will see it as a contribution to a task in which we are all involved – finding the way in which we need to understand and live the Christian faith in the rapidly changing conditions of our time.

Theology is not, of course, the only academic subject nor the church the only body in which such tensions and disagreements are to be found. They are a feature of every discipline that is concerned with the discovery of new knowledge, and of every institution that seeks to play a role in the world of its day. A few years ago, for example, the ranks of the astronomers were divided into bitterly competing factions, with the upholders of the big bang theory on the one side and the defenders of the steady state theory on the other. Similarly every political party has its deep divisions between hawks and doves, between theoreticians and pragmatists. Yet tensions of this kind impinge, so it seems to me, upon the theologian and upon the church in a peculiarly acute form. Why should that be? Let me suggest two basic reasons which arise directly from the nature of theology itself.

Theology is concerned with issues of deep personal faith. Those who feel it to be of importance at all (and that of course, as we know, is not everybody) feel it to be of fundamental importance to their own lives. It helps to provide a thought-out framework of belief, by which their lives can be sustained and directed at the deepest level of their being. Yet it is a part of the process of any academic discipline, as it searches for the way forward to new and more accurate delineations of its subject-matter, to prise open the agreed formulations of the past and to put all the available evidence on the rack of critical examination. And when theologians do that sort of thing to the substance of people's faith, they are bound to be accused not merely of trampling on people's dreams but of trampling on the most sacred reality of their waking lives. Where such a theologian works in a secular university and is also an ordained minister of the Christian church, the conflict is powerfully symbolized by the amphibious nature of his or her own existence. For such people live as it were in two worlds, however sure they may be that they are ultimately one. They are liable to be treated by their colleagues in the university as figures of faith, people whose faith is suspected of holding them back from making the most searching inroads into their subject and which may be thought to call into question the propriety of their position and of their subject's position in an open university. But at the same time and on the basis of the same activity they are liable to be treated by their colleagues in the church as figures of doubt, people whose questioning approach is felt to be incompatible with their membership of the church and their commission to preach the gospel. Little wonder if the tensions are acutely felt.

But I spoke of a second reason, arising similarly out of the fundamental nature of the subject. Theology is concerned with the ultimate realities of existence, with the infinite being of God. In scientific controversies, such as the one I referred to between the upholders of the big bang and steady state theories, the issues are of course difficult enough to resolve. If they were not, there would be no controversy. But in such cases, with advances in technology, it is always possible that new evidence may arise, or some crucial experiment may be devised, which will lead to decisive resolution of the particular issue at stake. That will not, of course, mean the end of all disagreement or of all controversy in the subject. New issues and new disputes will arise as research continues. But some issues of tension may come to receive more or less definitive solution. In other subjects, such as ethics or literary appreciation, this kind of general consensus is much more difficult to achieve. And in theology with its concern to speak about the mysteries of God, the difficulty of finding appropriate criteria for deciding between conflicting beliefs and interpretations is greater than ever. Uncertainties, and their consequent tensions, range over the whole field of the subject and are of long lasting duration.

To these two general reasons might well be added two of a more specific character, relating with particular force to our present situation. Critical historical study has been a marked feature of the last two hundred years and raises special problems for a faith which gives the crucial significance that Christianity has traditionally given to events that happened nearly two thousand years ago. And secondly our own century has seen the emergence of a world in which the claim of other faiths to be treated with equal seriousness alongside Christianity is very hard to resist. That development too raises special problems for a faith that has traditionally made the exclusivist kind of claim that has characterized Christianity. But for the moment I shall do no more than draw attention to these problems which I shall be discussing more fully in my second and third lectures. For the moment let us continue with the more general issues and with the way in which they have imposed themselves on the consciousness of the theologian and of Christians generally in the recent past.

For although all these problems are so integral to the very nature of theology and of faith that in one form or another they have always been there, nonetheless all of them – even the most general ones – arise today in a distinctive and increasingly acute form. You will have noticed that in my accounts of them I spoke of the position of the theologian in a secular university and compared the tensions that arise in the work of theology with those that characterize other academic disciplines. But the idea of the secular university and its insistence on a fully open spirit of enquiry are essentially modern concepts. It is the successful establishment of that sort of approach to knowledge in the world as a whole that highlights and intensifies the theologian's problem. It did not affect theologians so acutely in the past because it was then generally believed that there was available a source of knowledge about God which was immune from the kinds of problem and uncertainty that I have been describing. For the Catholic that source was located primarily in the teaching authority of the church; for the Protestant it was to be found in the absolute reliability of scripture. That did not of course mean that there was a cast-iron method of solution available for all problems or that no room was left for controversy. It doesn't need much knowledge of the history of the church to know that that was not the case. Tension and disagreement of the most violent kind could arise, for example, between Catholic and Protestant on the true interpretation of the words 'This is my body'. But even so the area in dispute was much more limited for them than it would be for the Christian scholar of today. They did not have to consider seriously the possibility that the words may not have been spoken by Jesus himself; or that if they were, they may not have been intended as part of a conscious institution of the eucharist; or that if they were so intended, they may have been drawing on thought-forms and categories inappropriate for our use today.

If we are to see clearly the nature of the situation in which we have to live and work, we need to recognize the way in which this belief in a privileged source of knowledge has had to change over the last hundred years. Let me illustrate it from the familiar story of changing attitudes to the authority of scripture. The year 1860 (the year immediately following that which saw the publication of Darwin's *Origin of Species*) saw the publication of another book, entitled *Essays and Reviews*. In it a group of Oxford scholars and churchmen sought to win acceptance in the Church of England for the steadily developing critical approach to scripture. By our standards the book does not appear very revolutionary stuff. Yet at the time it gave rise to a storm of protest. Indeed by the beginning of this century William Newton Clarke could look back on its appearance with just the same reaction. It 'created', he wrote, 'a stir that now seems incredible. At present it would seem gentle as a summer's breeze, but then it was a veritable storm-center in English theology!'[1] Its authors were denounced as the 'seven against Christ'. Liddon, who was to be Dean Ireland Professor of Exegesis in the University of Oxford, described them as 'men who were labouring to destroy and blot out the faith of Jesus Christ from the hearts of the English people'![2] And it was not a matter of words only. Some of the authors of *Essays and Reviews* suffered prosecution in the courts and condemnation in convocation. Yet the book had the effect its authors desired. Clarke records how it was a chance perusal of *Essays and Reviews* in a library that was the decisive moment in freeing him from the view that inspiration entailed inerrancy. And what happened to him, happened to many others. So gradually but inexorably the impossibility of the inerrancy view was established. It is symptomatic of the change that the Church of England underwent in the years that followed that before the nineteenth century was out one of the authors of *Essays and Reviews*, Frederick Temple, had been appointed Archbishop of Canterbury.

In retelling that story I have perhaps been less than fair to Liddon and to those who sided with him. I have painted him as a sheer reactionary, as a blind and obscurantist conservative.

Certainly the position he wanted to maintain was an impossible one. But were his anxieties wholly unjustified? Was not the acceptance of a critical approach to scripture, in however mild a form, the first step on a very slippery slope, an opening of the sluice gates? For if you can show that the Bible is not reliable at some points where we are in a position to check it, can we continue to rely on it at points where we are in no position to check it? And the crucial points where it speaks to us about the mind and purposes of God are precisely those where such checking is least open to us. Are we not thereby deprived of that special source of knowledge about God on which the church and Christian faith has depended in the past?

Some of you, I suspect, may be getting a bit impatient, may feel that I am making heavy weather of what I have myself described as a pretty familiar story. Does he really think, you may be asking yourselves, that we need to be weaned from a wholly uncritical and fundamentalist attitude to scripture? Have not the church and theological scholars succeeded in coming to terms with critical attitudes to scripture without the disasters that Liddon foretold overtaking us? Indeed they have. Yet I cannot wholly repress the fear that they may, in the words of the prophet Jeremiah, 'have healed the wound of my people lightly, saying "Peace, peace", when there is no peace' (Jer. 8.11). Or, to change the biblical allusion to the New Testament and direct the challenge to ourselves where it belongs, I fear lest, in condemning the obscurantists of the past and applauding the critically-minded pioneers of the nineteenth century, we may be like those Pharisees who are described as saying 'If we had lived in the days of our fathers, we would not have taken part with them in shedding the blood of the prophets' (Matt. 23.30). On which, you will remember, the ostensibly unfair comment of Jesus is given as 'thus you witness against yourselves that you are sons of those who murdered the prophets'. To be a true descendant of those who by their courageous advocacy of a critical approach to scripture a century ago helped to save the gospel for future generations, it is not enough to applaud their achievement; what is called for is that we should face with similar courage whatever may prove to be the analogous challenge of our own day. And that means that we have to ask whether the ways in which the church has come to terms so far with that first head-

on challenge to its earlier understanding of scripture will continue to provide as valid and effective an answer as they have
generally been thought to do until now. For I believe that there
were two main ways in which the church succeeded in assimilat-
ing the inescapable implications of criticism without serious dis-
location of her traditional faith. But I also believe that when we
examine those two ways carefully we shall find that both have to
face serious difficulties of their own. Let us then look at each of
them in turn.

1. The first way is that which goes under the general title of
'biblical theology'. It fully accepts the total collapse of the inerrancy approach, but claims that the Bible as a whole provides us
with a coherent picture of the human race as created by God and
redeemed through Christ. It is this general sense of the Bible,
this central theme of the biblical story that provides us with
what is needed for faith. Detailed accuracy is not important,
except in so far as it helps us to grasp these central motifs. But as
people have set about working out this approach in more detail,
two serious difficulties have arisen, of which the second is much
the more significant.

(*a*) The more closely one studies the Bible, the more aware
one becomes of the differences that exist, even within the New
Testament alone. In an appendix to the recent report of the
Church of England's Doctrine Commission, Christopher Evans
expressed himself in these terms. 'It is a real question whether
the accounts of the work and person of Jesus in the gospels of
Matthew, Mark, Luke and John can be legitimately added to one
another or combined to produce "the Christ".'[3] Of course there
is a measure of unity or homogeneity about the writings of the
New Testament, and one could argue at length about how most
fairly to describe the degree of difference within it. But if the
Bible were the only touchstone of Christian belief, it would certainly appear that a very wide variety of sets of belief could with
equal validity be derived from it.

(*b*) But the second difficulty is the one which seems to me to
be much the more far-reaching and it is this. There are several
underlying assumptions which are shared by virtually all the
New Testament writers, but which we neither do nor should nor
can share ourselves. I have in mind such things as demon pos-
session, the role of the miraculous or the expectation of an

apocalyptic end to the world by God's act. The point was force-
fully made in an article (by Lord Hailsham) in the *Times* (21
February 1976). His article was a response to the Doctrine Commission report to which I referred a moment ago, and in it he
wrote like this:

> Obviously the allegedly miraculous, whether it be the Virgin Birth,
> the feeding of the five thousand, or the resurrection itself, presents
> difficulties of credibility to the scientifically minded modern man.
> But far more serious to my mind is the time scale which the Bible
> presents, which underlies its whole view of human history. It is not
> the talking snake and the miraculous trees which puzzle one about
> the Genesis story of the creation, nor the difficulties of accommoda-
> tion in the overcrowded ark. These can easily be explained as alleg-
> ory or myth or a mixture of both. But to think of the world as about
> 6,000 years old enables the facts of the New Testament to be
> regarded easily as a culmination (as it was presented in the first
> century) or relatively easily as the prelude to a climax (which it has
> become between the second and the twentieth). But when it has
> come to be believed that the human race has been present on the
> planet for millions of years, and may, for aught we know, continue
> to be present for an indefinite time in the future, the uniqueness of
> the Christian religion requires to be demonstrated in quite a different
> way.

In other words, one can get over the particular difficulties which
loomed so large in the early debates about biblical criticism and
faith. One may even be able to deal with the internal varieties of
belief and understanding within the New Testament which Professor Evans' words so vividly illustrate. But it is the strangeness
of the Bible as a whole, the character of those assumptions that
all the New Testament writers shared with other people of their
age, which most distances it from us and means that it cannot be
as direct a guide to our believing as the biblical theologians had
led us to hope.

2. But I spoke also of a second way by which the church has
been able to absorb the shock of biblical criticism. That way I
would call the way of the creeds. This approach can accept
without any qualms both the variety and the strangeness of the
New Testament that I have been describing. For the ecumenical
creeds, so it claims, developed by the church in the early centuries of its life under the guidance of the Holy Spirit, enshrine
the essential and entirely trustworthy substance of Christian

belief. The route by which the church was led to them may turn out to be more circuitous than it had formerly appeared to be, but the goal to which she was rightly brought remains the same. Whatever historical oddities our studies may reveal on the way, 'the centre holds'. But here also there are two major difficulties to be faced, and once again it is the second which is the more serious of the two.

(a) In the first place there are particular clauses or affirmations of the creed which are not held to be true by all Christians and which it would be difficult to claim as essential tenets of Christian belief simply because they have found a place in the creeds. It is clear that there are some devout Christians and some leading Christian scholars who do not believe that Jesus was literally born of a virgin, in the sense that he was born without the normal means of sexual intercourse. Their assessment of the historical evidence for that ancient tenet of the faith simply does not allow them to affirm it with integrity. Yet the Virgin Birth is affirmed by the Apostles' Creed. An earlier Doctrine Commission of the Church of England, chaired by William Temple, acknowledged this fact in its 1938 report, but went on to say that this presented no grave problem because all members of the Commission, whatever their attitude to the Virgin Birth 'fully accepted the reality of our Lord's incarnation'.[4] In other words that Commission was treating the creeds in a way similar to that in which the biblical theologians were treating the Bible. It was not essential to maintain every detail, because the main point could continue to be maintained even when the detail (previously regarded as essential to the substantiation of the main point) was no longer believed.

(b) But it is precisely that analogy with the treatment of the Bible that alerts us to the second and more substantial difficulty. For if we accept that the creeds did not drop ready-made from heaven any more than the Bible, but that they, like the Bible, are products of their age, then are we not committed to a process of 'credal criticism' similar to the process of 'biblical criticism' that caused such heartaches to our ancestors of a hundred years ago? May not that be one of the fundamental tasks of our generation as biblical criticism was of theirs? When one looks at the assumptions and the arguments of those doctrinal debates out of which the creeds emerged, it is hard to resist the conclusion that the world of the creeds is a stranger to us almost as much as the world of the Bible. The age of the creeds is the period to which most of my own specialist study has been directed, and the conviction to which such study has led me is certainly that it is more natural and more reasonable to see the creeds and the categories of thought in which they are enshrined as a product of their age than to see them as changeless truths to be maintained in all subsequent ages. This means that even with such a fundamental concept as the incarnation of the pre-existent Son of God we may need to ask whether it is something that is an inalienable element of Christianity as such or whether it may not be a category appropriate to the expression of Christian faith then, but not necessarily binding on Christian theology today. That is a question rather than an affirmation. Moreover it is a question to which the answer is not obvious. If it was, there would not, as I said at the outset of the lecture, be the kind of tension and disagreement that in fact surrounds the work of the critical theologian today. What I have tried to do thus far is to show why I think such questions are bound to arise, and why the critical theologian has some ground for regarding the raising of them not merely as a regrettable if inevitable necessity but as constituting a constructive contribution to the life of the church.

It is this possibility which it is vital for the church to acknowledge. For in practice the response of the critical theologian's more conservative colleagues is liable to go something like this: 'Is it not intolerably arrogant for you to say (as you certainly appear to be saying) that for two thousand years Christianity has lived by the faith that is enshrined in the creeds but that now you in your cleverness have detected a flaw at the very heart of that faith? Admittedly traditional faith has rightly been submitted to criticism in the past. But the situation there was different. A geocentric universe, a special creation of man, the literal truth of the Bible, even the Virgin Birth – none of these was essential to the faith. But the things that you are calling into question now touch the faith at its very heart.' To this very understandable challenge, the critical theologian can and should reply in some such way as this: 'Your remarks seem to me to betray lack of a proper sense of historical imagination. To people like Liddon, as I've already shown, the literal truth of the Bible appeared to be the necessary condition of Christian faith. And even in this century a highly sophisticated Christian thinker, like J. N. Figgis, could write of thé Virgin Birth in the Preface to his Hulsean Lectures: "I have found as a fact that if we attempt to live with that doctrine cut off from the faith, it is all up with Christianity."[5] Is it not then you who are (unconsciously, of course) being guilty of arrogance? For you are bound to recognize that time and again in the past people have claimed that some aspect of the faith was essential and irreformable, while subsequent generations have come to acknowledge that it was not (in its earlier form at least) as essential or as irreformable as had been claimed. Yet you appear to be claiming that now in the twentieth century you are in a position to delineate just what is essential to Christian faith and ought not to be called into question.'

Such a response should not, of course, be understood to suggest that the more untraditional a theologian's view the more likely it is to be right. Such a suggestion would be utterly absurd. But it is to suggest that when theologians call into question established beliefs, even beliefs of great importance in the inherited structure of the faith, they are not on that score alone to be regarded as automatically wrong. But even if all that be admitted it might still seem that the role I have been attributing to the critical theologian is a discouragingly negative one. Grant the soundness of the argument, and does not the theologian's role become one of a gradual dismantling of the edifice of faith? And if that really were the case, ought not the theologian to resist it like Churchill when he said he had not been appointed to preside over the break-up of the British Empire? The example itself points to a very different answer that the theologian ought to give. For the so-called break-up of the British Empire (symbolized in that case by the granting of independence to India) can also be seen more positively as the creation of the Commonwealth. What the theologian helps to dismantle are particular statements of faith that may have been appropriate to the knowledge and culture of a different age or for which a greater degree of precision and certainty had been claimed than it is given us to enjoy. Take away belief in a special creation of the human race and the doctrine of the creation of men and women in the image of God does not simply disappear; rather the way is opened up to re-develop and re-express it in a religiously more satisfying form. Take away belief in the inerrancy of scripture and you do not abolish the role of scripture for Christian faith; rather the way is opened up for a truer and more profound understanding of it. The work of demolition goes hand-in-hand with the more positive work of theological construction.

I am not suggesting that it is easy or that it does no damage. Such a process is disturbing, it is unsettling. And the theologian ought not to be surprised if some people in the church resist it passionately. Is there not enough unsettling change in the world around us? And is not religious faith concerned with the unchanging, a proper source of security in this uncertain and transient world? Indeed it is. But the only ultimate security is in God himself. Other things – buildings, institutions, formularies – may help to mediate the reality of God's eternal changeless-ness to us. But none of them, however good, must be allowed the absoluteness that belongs to God alone. That is idolatry. Indeed the more sacrosanct the thing may be, the greater the danger of idolatry. 'If any man comes to me,' said Jesus, 'and does not hate his own father and mother and wife and children and brothers and sisters, yea, and even his own life, he cannot be my disciple' (Luke 14.26). The point of the saying is not that family ties and family affection are bad; indeed if that were so, the saying would lose its point. It is precisely because they are the highest of human goods that they are in danger of being given the absolute devotion that belongs only to God.

So it is with our beliefs. They never fully express the truth that is God. So theologians who challenge them need not necessarily be undermining faith. They may in the long run be helping us to direct it more appropriately to its proper object, namely God himself. Faith is not believing things we know to be untrue, nor believing them with a confidence the evidence does not warrant. It is a way of response to the God whom we cannot know with certainty. So doubt is not always the enemy of faith; it is endemic to our human situation, and can have a corrective and purifying role within the life of faith. Theology is the attempt to co-ordinate faith and doubt in a way which does justice to our status as responsible human beings, in a way that seeks to save us from the short cuts alike of superstitious credulity and of despairing scepticism.

So although the work of the critical theologian today is likely to cut deep and to be disturbing to many, it ought not to be seen as something that stands in opposition to the faith of the church. In this lecture I have tried to show in general terms how it may rather be something of vital importance to the life of the church. In the second and third lectures I shall attempt to suggest the form it may need to take in the two important areas of christology and of Christianity's relation to other faiths.

2

Christology in an Age of Historical Studies

The field of christology is more like a minefield than like any
other kind of field. The records of the early history of the church
are strewn with accounts of those who have come to grief in it –
Arians and Apollinarians, Nestorians and Eutychians, Mono-
physites and Monothelites. But the problem with which I want
to begin this lecture is one that lies behind any such particular
problems. What is the proper subject matter of christology?
What is it really about? Since the form of the word is Greek and
the early history of the Greek-speaking churches of the East is
the most important period for christological thought it comes as
something of a surprise to discover that the Greek form
Χριστολογία does not appear in Liddell and Scott or in Lampe's
Patristic Lexicon. Less common English words, like christolatry
and christomaniac, have their Greek equivalents in Χριστολάτ-
ρης and Χριστομανία but not christology. Strange words like
Χριστοκάπηλος which is defined as meaning 'making Christ a
subject for business deals' appear in the lexicon, but not Χριστολογία. So no direct help is forthcoming from that quarter.

Christology is not just a matter of interpreting the figure of
Jesus; it is not Jesuology which is at the heart of Christian theology. (Just as, it is worth noting in passing, scholars of Buddh-
ism speak sometimes of Buddhology but never, so far as I am
aware, of Gautamology.) But nor is christology simply a study of
the Messianic idea, as its etymological derivation might suggest;
its subject includes both Jesus of Nazareth and the risen Lord of
the church's faith, whether apprehended under messianic or
other categories. In the jargon language of theological scholarship, a language which I fear sometimes helps us to evade rather

than come to terms with the real issues, it is concerned both with the Jesus of history and the Christ of faith. But the nature of the identity between those two is precisely part of our problem. Thus there is a fundamental elusiveness about the basic subject matter of christology. It is not a case of the questions being clear but the answers hard to find; it is hard even to be clear about the questions. The connotation of the word 'Christ' is not simple, nor can we simplify it without prejudging the issue. Its complexity must be retained and kept firmly in mind. For if we overlook it, we shall soon find that in the course of any discussion the object of reference itself is shifting in a way that stultifies and invalidates our argument.

But my concern in this lecture is not with the impossibly wide topic of christology in all its varied manifestations but with the perhaps still impossibly wide topic of the impact on christology of modern historical thinking. Historical study has implications for every aspect of christology, but it obviously impinges with particular force on that part of it which relates most directly to the historical figure of Jesus. And I want to begin by tracing that impact in terms of the more general account of recent theological development that I gave in the previous lecture. So let me first briefly recall the structure of that analysis. I began with the breakdown in the nineteenth century of any possible appeal to scripture as a source of inerrant knowledge about God. I then considered the alternative approach of biblical theology and emphasized the twin difficulties of the diversity of the Bible and the strangeness of the biblical world-view. Finally I mentioned the appeal to creeds and there too stressed two difficulties – doubts about particular clauses on the one hand and about the broad interpretative categories of that early credal tradition on the other. Thus there were five stages or five forms in which I saw the historical study so characteristic of the nineteenth and twentieth centuries putting a challenge to the accepted patterns of Christian belief – the challenge to inerrancy, the challenges of diversity and strangeness, and the challenges to particular credal affirmations and to the broader framework of credal thought. Let us now look at the implications of those five challenges for the more specific topic of christology.

1. One of those nineteenth-century conservatives who viewed with grave disquiet the oncoming tide of biblical criticism was

the immensely learned Regius Professor of Modern History and later Bishop of Oxford, William Stubbs. He felt particular alarm at the application of such critical method not just to the Old Testament but to the gospel records themselves. It seemed to him to be a first step towards 'the day when the Church shall cry out to Jesus of Nazareth "Thou hast deceived me and I was deceived"'.[1] For one of the corollaries of a traditional christology with its direct identification of Jesus of Nazareth with the coequal Son of God has been the conviction, held throughout much of the church's history, that in the words of Jesus we have been given incorrigible information about such fundamental questions as Jesus' special relationship to God and the nature of life after death, and binding instructions on such issues as the need for baptism in the threefold name and the inadmissibility of divorce.In my experience the anxiety felt by Bishop Stubbs is still felt by many members of the church. It is not uncommon to meet with the feeling that something is badly amiss if the words of Jesus are not regarded as having immediate and absolute authority for us today. But though the gospel records, of course, and the recorded words of Jesus in particular continue to be of special importance to the church, our knowledge of the general way in which the gospel tradition was transmitted makes it impossible for us legitimately to treat them as the direct voice of God to us, however traditional our christological convictions may continue to be.

2. One of the difficulties about taking the recorded teaching of Jesus on divorce as absolutely binding has always been that the Matthean Jesus and the Markan Jesus do not appear to say the same thing, and only by the most implausible exegetical *tour de force* can they be made to say the same thing. That fact points us to the second problem – the diversity of the New Testament pictures of Jesus as a whole. Let me repeat those words of Professor Evans which I quoted last time, since they relate particularly to christology. 'It is a real question', he wrote, 'whether the accounts of the work and person of Jesus in the gospels of Matthew, Mark, Luke and John can be legitimately added to one another or combined to produce "the Christ".'[2] In other words, no sooner have we freed ourselves from an infantile longing for an oracular Christ who will provide us with infallible information and instructions about the basic issues of life, and have

turned to look in a broader and more mature way for a Christ who embodies the spirit of fully authentic human life, than we are faced with the fact that no such single figure may be available to us. This may make more explicable the fact that down the ages people have found so many different models of Christlikeness on the basis of the same set of records – an ascetic and a worldly Christ, a pacifist and a revolutionary Jesus and so on. All have some roots in the records of Jesus; none squares with all the evidence. But if this helps to make past confusion more understandable, it does not seem to provide us with much help out of that confusion today.

3. But we have to reckon not only with the problem of finding a single, coherent Christ on the basis of the records of the life of Jesus. A further problem is whether any Christ we might conceivably discover by such means would be intelligible, attractive or convincing to us; or whether he would be so much imbued with the attitudes and expectations of his age that he would inevitably remain something of a stranger to us today. This was the conclusion to which Schweitzer came at the end of his famous study of the nineteenth-century quest of the historical Jesus. The aim of that quest had been to 'bring Jesus straight into our times as Teacher and Saviour'. It succeeded in loosing 'the bands by which He had been riveted for centuries to the stony rocks of ecclesiastical doctrine' and reached the point of seeing 'life and movement coming into the figure once more, and the historical Jesus advancing, as it seemed to meet it. But He does not stay; He passes by our time and returns to His own ... by the same inevitable necessity by which the liberated pendulum returns to its original position'.[3] We do not need to share in full Schweitzer's apocalyptic understanding of Jesus to agree that if we take history seriously, if we are not crypto-Gnostics at heart, the Jesus-component of our Christ figure is likely to be an uncomfortable alien in our contemporary world.

4. The fourth area of questioning which I raised last time related to particular articles of the creed, and I took as an example the Virgin Birth. So far in this lecture I have been stressing that historical study tends to reveal a Jesus who as a citizen of the first century is something of a stranger to our own ideals of human knowledge and human expectations. In those areas of life where we have been inclined to see him as very like our-

selves, only immeasurably greater, I have been stressing his difference from us. But there have always been other things about Jesus, like his miraculous powers, which have consciously separated him from us. The Virgin Birth is one example of sufficient importance to find a place in the creed. This essential difference contributed to his being seen not simply as one of us, but as one with us with a difference – a difference that made all the difference. Even in his incarnate life he was the supernatural Christ, able because of who he was to break once for all the entail of sin, to ransom the world from the power of Satan. But once admit that the New Testament documents must be submitted to the scrutiny of critical historical assessment, and the miraculous events, which historically have been so important a part of the grounds for belief in a supernatural Christ, become much more problematical. One does not need to be a thorough-going physical determinist to claim that once the New Testament has been set alongside other literature of its own age and its writings assessed in the manner characteristic of normal historical work, it becomes very difficult to go on affirming, for example, the Virgin Birth as an event in history deserving firm credence.

5. But, as I said in the previous lecture, the problem with which we are faced in relation to credal doctrine is not simply a matter of particular clauses, like the Virgin Birth. When that has been affirmed as of vital importance, it has normally been because it was regarded as an integral part of belief in Jesus as incarnate. And there are those today, as there were when William Temple's Doctrine Commission was meeting fifty years ago, who would withold belief in the virginal conception of Jesus but who would still express faith in him as the incarnation of a pre-existent divine being, the eternal and co-equal Son of God. That at least, it might seem, is a claim free from the uncomfortable challenge of historical studies. For it is a religious or metaphysical claim rather than a directly historical one. In that respect it differs from the Virgin Birth or the physical resurrection of Jesus. That is true. Yet historical study is not wholly irrelevant. What it can do and what it does do is to throw light on the way in which this dominant motif of virtually all subsequent theology arose. In the first place it enables us to see that traditional christology bears a much less straightforward rela-

tionship to the New Testament evidence than has generally been assumed in the past. In the words of James Dunn, 'what many Christians both past and present have regarded as orthodox christology may be represented (not altogether unfairly) as a curious amalgam of different elements taken from different parts of first-century Christianity – personal pre-existence from John, virgin birth from Matthew, the miracle worker from the so-called 'divine man' christology prevalent among some Hellenistic Christians, his death as atonement from Paul, the character of his resurrection from Luke, his present role from Hebrews and the hope of his parousia from the earlier decades.'[4] None of these strands (not even the Fourth Gospel) fully corresponds to the affirmation of later orthodoxy. There was a further stage of development in the centuries that followed. Recent historical study has given us a fuller and more accurate picture of that process of development than was available to the church in the past. It helps us to see how the reasoning employed drew upon contemporary assumptions about the nature of scripture or about the role of heavenly beings and intermediaries of a kind that the great majority of Christians today do not share. Such historical reflections do not, of course, disprove the traditional credal doctrine of incarnation. As I said at the outset of the discussion, it would be absurd in the nature of the case to suggest that they should. But they do, as it seems to me, suggest that it might be more reasonable for us to see it as an interpretation of Jesus appropriate to its own age rather than as a truth binding on all subsequent generations.[5]

Where then do these reflections lead us? In, it may well seem to some of you, a depressingly negative direction. For what I have been suggesting in terms of the five stages that we have been following is that, if Jesus of Nazareth is a component part of the Christ in whom we believe, then historical study decisively disproves the possibility of an infallible Christ, seriously undermines the availability of a single, coherent Christ or of an intelligible, twentieth-century Christ, and finally puts a question mark against the grounds for belief in a supernatural or incarnate Christ. But do not despair. One does not have to be a Hegelian to believe that a lecture should not consist simply of thesis, but should have its element of antithesis too. What then may be said by way of antithesis?

Although for reasons of brevity I have had to make my points rather dogmatically, what I have set before you so far is how I see the impact of historical study on christology. It is not, of course, how all critically minded theologians see the matter. Most of those who see its implications as less profoundly challenging than I do, are only able to do so, so it seems to me, because they do not really take critical historical study seriously enough. By one means or another, which seem to me unjustified, they blunt the sharpness of its challenge when they come to apply it to scripture or to the main tradition of the church's faith. One scholar of whom that general criticism can not fairly be made but whose conclusions are very different from my own is Wolfhart Pannenberg. It is a basic principle of scholarship that when one finds someone whose method appears sound and whose learning is impeccable but whose final position strongly conflicts with one's own, there one has someone whose work one must take with great seriousness. How then does Pannenberg conclude that on the basis of the most rigorously critical historical scholarship, it is possible to continue to affirm a christology in the closest continuity with that of the main church tradition down the ages?

His argument goes something like this. On critical grounds we can establish that the heart of Jesus' proclamation was the imminence of the end of the world and the general resurrection of the dead. This did not happen as predicted. What did happen was the resurrection of Jesus alone – an occurrence which can properly be affirmed on the basis of normal historical argument. That happening, understood within the context of the late Jewish apocalyptic expectation of the general resurrection, constituted a proleptic presence of the end of history. For that reason the resurrection of Jesus reveals a substantial presence of God in him, which because of the relativity of history could not properly be affirmed of him otherwise. Nevertheless because what was true of him in his resurrection has retroactive force, it is therefore true of him also throughout his ministry, though wholly unknown then even to Jesus himself.[6] I have drastically, but I hope not unfairly, compressed a highly complex and subtle argument. What I want to emphasize is this. To establish his case, Pannenberg has to commit himself in three ways which seem to me to ride somewhat roughshod over the kinds of difficulty I have been outlining. First he has to begin from one particular reconstruction of the message of Jesus – the proclamation of the imminence of the general resurrection. This is a plausible historical reconstruction, but only one among a variety of such possible reconstructions. Then secondly he has to claim that the resurrection of Jesus can properly be affirmed, not on the basis of faith about who Jesus was because it is required as the basis for that faith, but by normal historical means. That would take too long to argue out here, but I do not find myself able to agree with him at that point.[7] And thirdly, even if we have surmounted that difficulty, we have to be able to take the apocalyptic outlook of first-century Judaism seriously, not merely as the historical setting of the teaching of Jesus but as a presupposition of our own believing too. Though that does not imply trying to make the imagery of apocalyptic our own, it does involve being convinced that 'the form of apocalyptic thought ... corresponds to the true form of human existence' that 'its essential meaning is foreign to no culture'. Even with that qualification I find myself unable to go with him on this third point also.[8] So the outcome of my own engagement with Pannenberg's thought is to conclude that his impressive attempt to re-establish a fully traditional christology explicitly on the basis of a thorough-going critical historical method does not finally succeed. It does not take full enough account of the variety of plausible reconstructions of the teaching of Jesus, of the problems faced by historical study in relation to reports of such utterly exceptional events as the resurrection or the difficulty of taking the apocalyptic hope – or some supposed equivalent to it – as the framework for determining our own beliefs today.

So far then my promised antithesis has not got very far off the ground. I have reminded you that not all critically minded scholars find the challenge of historical study to christology as far reaching as I do. But of that no doubt you were well aware already. I have not succeeded in drawing from the work of Pannenberg, much as I admire it, anything that can contribute to a positive exposition of christology in the face of historical study. Where else can we turn?

Christology is not Christianity. Christology is the church's attempt to give some unified account of Jesus of Nazareth and of its apprehension of God through him in the experience of Christian faith. If the traditional patterns of christological doctrine should succumb to the challenges of historical study, that does not mean that Jesus of Nazareth would cease to be of significance for the life of the church nor that the experience of God through him would be destroyed. Recall Schweitzer's words about the aim of the original quest of the historical Jesus to 'loose the bands by which He had been riveted for centuries to the stony rocks of ecclesiastical doctrine'. Can the contemporary challenge of historical study to christology be seen in a similar way, not as destructive of faith but as having a potential to bring new life to the figure of Jesus and to Christian experience in our own time?

Let me begin my attempt at a constructive statement, as I began my critical assessment, with Jesus. Jesus of Nazareth was a historical figure and is known to us primarily through the records of the New Testament. All the gospels are interpretative accounts, and while we can draw some distinctions between 'history' and 'interpretation', between what goes back to Jesus and what is a subsequent development of the early church, in the nature of the case most distinctions of that kind are bound to remain tentative and inconclusive.

The first century saw the founding of the church and radical changes in man's apprehension of God. For that we have first-hand evidence. And it is to that overall movement of which we have first-hand evidence that scholars are referring when they speak in their ugly jargon of 'the Christ event'. That is not to deny the importance of Jesus himself. That he was the prime creative force in that historic movement of change seems to me beyond question. But the exact nature of that prime creative force, of his specific contribution, is something of which we can be much less confident. A considerable degree of doubt on that score is simply a fact of life with which we have to learn to live.

This lack of knowledge about the precise character of Jesus himself and of his teaching does nothing to prevent us reflecting on the pictures of Jesus presented to us in the various gospel records and finding vividly depicted there certain characteristics of fundamental religious significance – a sense of God's immediacy to the world and to himself, openness toward God and other men, trust in God and a sense of being commissioned by him, forgivingness and faithfulness through suffering even to the point of death. The strangeness of that world of which Jesus was a part, to which I referred earlier, does not mean that he or his world are wholly opaque to us. We can recognize and respond to such basic human characteristics in the story as I have just described, even when the specific beliefs that accompanied them or forms of life in which they were expressed are very different from our own. Admittedly we need to acknowledge that any such description is liable to involve some element of distortion, a tendency to select those things that will make Jesus conform to our ideals, but that fact does not render it wholly arbitrary or valueless. Moreover, the consistency between life and teaching in the gospel accounts of Jesus enables them to rise above the didactic level and to focus the religious vision in a personal form – something of the utmost importance for their living religious significance. These pictures of Jesus, the first-century Rabbi of Nazareth, cannot be straightforwardly the model for all subsequent human living. Nevertheless there is in the pictures that we are given of him a sufficient concentration of central motifs in a sufficiently vivid form for them to continue to play a creative and a corrective role in relation to subsequent human ideals.

Whenever in the past people have thought themselves able to find an absolute guide to conduct in the human life of Jesus, just because it was the human life of the Son of God, they were inevitably involved in a measure of self-deception. For in interpreting and applying that human life to their own situation, there was always an element of selection and of distortion involved in the process of making that gospel ideal applicable to their own age. What I have done is to emphasize the impossibility of that life serving as such an absolute ideal, but at the same time I have also emphasized its continuing value as a creative and corrective component in the complex process of determining our basic religious and moral attitudes. If historical study has helped us to see more clearly what has always in fact been the nature of people's relation to the gospel story, then it has done us a service for which we should be grateful.

But all that I have said so far relates only to what we traditionally call the 'humanity' of Christ. And it is his 'divinity' that has been of paramount significance for the life of faith. What is to be said on that score? If we should come to the conclusion that the understanding of Jesus as the incarnation of the Second Person of the Trinity was a way of understanding him that was appropriate in a past era but that no longer carried the same conviction today, would we have simply to abandon all the wealth of religious meaning that that concept has conveyed in the past? If that were so, it would indeed be a negative and destructive conclusion. But I do not believe that it is so. What was this specialness of Jesus that traditional teaching has interpreted in incarnational terms? One way in which we might answer that question is this. He was not just one who had taught about God; he was not just one who had lived a life of perfect human response to God. He had lived a life that embodied and expressed God's character and action in the world. As prophets in the past had expressed the word of God that had come to them not only in speech but also in symbolic action, so in a far more comprehensive way did Jesus. The impact not merely of his teaching but of his whole person communicated the presence and the power of God with an unprecedented sense of directness and finality. Incarnational language was a very effective way of expressing this conviction about him. Treat that language in a strict, metaphysical way (as the mainstream of Christian tradition has done) so that the acts of Jesus are understood as in some more direct sense to be God's acts and we are faced with difficulties of understanding that seem to me in the last resort insuperable. None of the innumerable ways in which the church has assayed to meet that challenge in the past or in which it does so today seems to me to escape the charge either of logical incoherence, or of undermining the genuineness of the humanity of Jesus.[9]

But that is not the only way in which to treat the language. We can also regard it as a form of poetic or mythological language. There is nothing very new in that suggestion, but a lot of work still needs to be done before we can claim to have any satisfactory elaboration of what it involves. Historical studies have so dominated the approach of theological work in the recent past, that mythological interpretation has too often been seen in a negative light, as standing in direct conflict with historical interpretation. Where that danger has been avoided, the concept of myth has often been used so loosely that it has ceased to be a useful tool of interpretation. Theologians need perhaps to go to school with the literary critics as thoroughly as they have done with the historical critics, before a more positive and more controlled development of what would be involved in such an approach will emerge. For Christianity is rooted both in events and in imaginative interpretation of events. It is a religion of history and of a book. The approach of the historical critic and of the literary critic need to be used together in the work of theological understanding. But it is my belief that when this is done incarnational language understood in a properly mythological way will prove to be a powerful pictorial way of affirming the most fundamental truths about God's ways with the world. For in the life of the Jesus who ate with publicans and sinners and who endured ultimately death on a cross, if we understand it in this way, we have an enacted parable of the love that embraces all people and will not let them go, of the God who unites people to himself in a relationship of the most intimate union, who shares their sufferings and holds them even in and through the tragedy of death. [10]

Such a vision is not, of course, a conclusion of critical historical study. It is, as any Christian position is bound to be, a bold but not ungrounded act of faith. But it may be able to lay claim to this advantage. It has looked firmly in the face the implications of critical historical study both about the gospels and about the development of doctrine in the formative early church period. It acknowledges the inevitable uncertainty that appertains to our knowledge of events in the distant past and the great difference of world-view that separates that age from our own. And having done that it comes out with a faith in God whose fundamental character still has important links of continuity with some of the central themes in the church's traditional understanding of God and of his purposes for the world. It is true that the historical problems it encounters, together with certain philosophical difficulties for our contemporary speech about God, may hold it back from producing any christology in the traditional sense of that word. But thay may not be as serious a lack as it sounds at first hearing, if by a christology of the traditional kind we mean one that speaks of a special ontological relationship between Jesus and God. For, as we saw at the outset of this lecture, the precise subject matter of christology is hard to tie down and the various concerns that have usually come under its umbrella may prove to be more accurately and effectively dealt with in other and separate ways.

Let me put the problem this way. The Son of God of Mark 14.36 who prays 'Abba, Father, take away this cup from me, nevertheless not my will but thine be done' is a human son standing in that Jewish tradition where the essential characteristic of sonship is perfect obedience to the will of God. The Son of God of John 1.18 who is in the bosom of the Father and makes known the unseen and the unseeable God is the revelatory pole of the mysterious God who is both hidden and self-revealing. The two are not unrelated to one another. And if one thinks that 'Son of God' in the New Testament and in Christian theology is a univocal term, then one will relate them to one another by way of identity of personal being. Or in other words one will relate them to one another by way of a christology. But to regard 'Son of God' as a univocal term in that way is a large and not very plausible assumption. If one does not make it, then there will be other ways in which those two convictions can be correlated with one another. For example the concept of the Johannine Son might be seen as part of an imaginative and pictorial account of the mystery of the divine being which provides an interpretative context within which the records of Jesus and of his enactment of the way of God can be set. In other words they would be related to one another within the setting of a *theo*logy or a theology of history rather than of a christology. For to relate them by constructing any kind of christology is to commit oneself to one particular way of co-ordinating the evidence with which we begin: it is not the only way, nor am I convinced that it is the best way. Some of the questions and the issues that traditionally figure in the theological textbook under the heading of christology will no longer arise (and their disappearance would be no loss); others will reappear under different headings and new light on them may come from their changed environment. Whether in the long run the kind of historical difficulty that I have outlined in this lecture will come to be felt more and more widely (as, for example, the difficulties about traditional accounts of Christian faith that were set in train by the discovery of evolution have done), only time will tell. What I as a critical theologian want to say to the church at this point is this: 'If that does happen,' (as I suspect it will, though my expectation may prove to be mistaken) 'could the kind of attitude to Jesus and to incarnational christology that I have sketched here in bare out-line perhaps provide a positive way forward for the church in such a situation?' It is offered in the hope that it might – indeed in the hope that it might prove not merely an acceptable alterna-tive, but even in some respects a preferable one. One respect in which that might well turn out to be the case is the relation of Christianity to other faiths. And of that I shall be speaking in my third lecture.

3

Christian Theology in an Age of Religious Studies

Not even the most intrepid apologist for the Christian faith is likely to claim that the record of Christianity's dealings with other faiths is a very happy story. Many of the sentiments expressed and the actions committed in the course of that story are a source of shock and embarrassment to the contemporary Christian. Some of its unhappier episodes may be attributed to what modern ecumenical jargon calls 'non-theological factors' – individual human failings that characterize Christians as well as others. To say that is not to excuse them; it is a part of the necessary task of trying to understand them. Some are due to factors that may broadly be described as sociological. Human groups often derive their sense of cohesion and purpose by setting some other group over against themselves and treating that group as a scapegoat or common enemy. The church has done that over long periods of time in relation both to Judaism and to Islam. Such factors might be dubbed semi-theological. They do not arise directly out of the nature of the faith itself, though they do perhaps raise questions about how far the church should seek to function as one human group amongst others. But that is a complex question that I do not want to pursue today. For some of the attitudes and incidents that give rise to our sense of shock and embarrassment derive from factors of a fully theological character; they arise directly out of convictions at the heart of the Christian faith of those involved. It is with these that I shall be particularly concerned.

It is not hard to pin-point the Christian conviction that most directly leads to a negative evaluation of other religions. It can provisionally be indicated by the citation of two New Testament texts – the words of Peter in Acts 4.12 'There is salvation in no one else, for there is no other name under heaven given to the world by which we must be saved' and the words of Jesus himself according to the Fourth Gospel in John 14.6 'I am the way, the truth and the life; no one comes to the Father but by me'. The way in which such texts have often, and not altogether unnaturally, been understood is frightening. For many generations of devout Christians have been convinced that the God of love whom they worshipped would condemn to eternal punishment all those who had never called on the name of Jesus, whether they had ever heard that name or not. Usually so harsh a doctrine has been mitigated in one way or another, though the repercussions of those mitigations have not always been entirely reassuring. I remember as a student hearing Bertrand Russell recount a meeting with a missionary in China. The missionary prided himself on holding the enlightened view that hell was not for those who had never heard the name of Jesus but only for those who had heard and rejected it. But since he was himself working in a difficult pioneer area, the fruit of his life's work was the making of a handful of converts – say 100 out of some 10,000 to whom he had preached. So, as it seemed to Russell, the result of all his labours had been to send 9,900 souls to hell. In such a context other religions are seen as rivals or deceivers, the work of devils leading people astray to their eternal ruin. Such views, of course, are crude in the extreme, but we need to recall how widely they have been held in Christian history, as we seek to understand the attempts of Christian theology to define a more possible and more palatable position.

The title of this lecture speaks of our age as an age of religious studies. By this I mean that we live in an age in which religions are studied not simply because they are believed to be false, so that the Christian apologist may be able to refute them with greater effectiveness; nor simply because they are believed to be true, so that the evangelist may expound his or her own faith with greater understanding; but also because, whatever their truth or falsity, they are seen as potent influences in the life of mankind or profound flowerings of the human spirit, worthy of interest and study for their own sakes. It is within the context of such studies that Christians have to review their attitude to other faiths and Christian theology to assess the implications of these changes for its own understanding of its own faith. The full force of the development of religious studies for the Christian theologian is sometimes obscured when in practice the study of religions becomes the study of religions other than Christianity. Where Christian theology is already in existence as a distinct subject of study, there may be administrative arguments in favour of such a procedure. But it is a dangerously misleading one. Christianity is a religion, and it is important that in the study of religions it should be included alongside other faiths.

To say that Christianity is a religion may seem so obvious a remark that it hardly needs saying. Yet one response of some Christian theologians to the emergence of an age of religious studies was precisely to deny that Christianity is a religion. The classic expression of such a position was Kraemer's *The Christian Message in a non-Christian World*.[1] In effect that position is a sophisticated attempt to perpetuate some of the worst elements in Christian attitudes. That harshly critical judgment of the contrast between Christian 'gospel' and human 'religion' seems to me inescapable when one reads claims such as that made by Dr Schlink in an article published in the *International Review of Missions* in 1938 (the same year as the publication of Kraemer's book) and drawing explicitly on the work of Kraemer and of Barth. 'On the one side', he wrote, 'stands God's words and acts; on the other man's quest and labour; on one side the eternal truth of saving love; on the other, the daemonic impulse to picture God in one's own image and to make Him subservient to one's own will. . . . Any attempt to make links with them would be to make links with lies and deception.'[2] I do not propose to argue with that position. Not because I dislike its conclusions (which I do), but because its basic premise is so patently false. Whatever else Christianity is, it is a religion, and only someone blinded by his own cleverness could be fool enough to claim that it was not.

But one does not have to descend to such expedients to make out a case for the continuing uniqueness of Christian faith in an age of religious studies. Many serious and sensitive scholars have done so without recourse to such question-begging methods. Their main line of argument is to claim that Christians have often been at fault in the past in seeking to maintain an exclusive view of the uniqueness of Christ and of the Christian faith; whereas what should be insisted on is not an exclusive, but an inclusive view of that uniqueness. What are the implications and what is the validity of this line of argument?

The assessment that we make of the character of the Fourth Gospel is one of the main factors in determining the precise form of that impact of historical studies on our christology that I was discussing in the last lecture. This can be seen with particular clarity in relation to the Johannine text I quoted just now. Treat the words 'no one comes to the Father but by me' as words of Jesus of Nazareth and the implications that our forebears found in them are not easy to resist. But coming in the Fourth Gospel, they come as words spoken by one who is explicitly the embodiment of the eternal Logos, the light who enlightens everyone. The way is thus left wide open for a more charitable attitude towards other faiths. They may indeed contain substantial glimpses of truth, derived from the divine Logos. But whatever truth they contain will also be found more fully present in Christ, because he is the Logos incarnate.

This approach is no new invention, specially thought up to cope with a modern problem. It is also to be found as early as the second century in such a writer as Justin Martyr. Though Justin admittedly saw much ancient religion as deliberate demonic imitation of the truth designed to entrap the unwary, he also spoke of people like Socrates as Christians before Christ because their wisdom came from partial apprehension of the same Logos that was fully embodied in Jesus. And this approach has remained as a kind of minority report in the church down the ages. Erasmus is reported to have included the petition when 'telling his beads': 'Sancte Socrates, Ora pro nobis!'[3]

This approach has not proved as attractive to adherents of other faiths as its proponents could have wished. They may have recognized it as more charitable, but it has seemed to them to be charitable in the pejorative sense of that word. It has a patronizing and condescending ring. What is good in their faiths is good only because it is more fully present in Christianity. But more important than whether it has proved popular is whether such an approach can make out a good case for being true. And here, despite wide support among critically minded Christian scholars, it seems to me to run into grave difficulties.

The difficulties are centred on the issue, to which I referred in the last lecture, of the identity of Jesus and the Logos. For if the Christian claim were that every positive insight of other faiths was already present to the mind of Jesus or implied by his religious outlook, it would I think be clearly false. If on the other hand it takes the form of saying that every positive insight must derive from the Logos and, since Jesus was the Logos incarnate, it belongs in a fuller and more fundamental sense to Christ and the religion that acknowledges him, then it is no more than a tautology. On this argument since all good comes from the Logos and Jesus is the Logos incarnate we can know in advance that every good belongs to him, whatever the empirical evidence.

I can perhaps make clearer what I mean in calling this revised form of the Christian claim a tautology by comparing it with the very similar problem that arises in relation to Roman Catholic teaching about the church. At one time the saying 'No salvation outside the church' was understood in a straightforward way to mean that salvation was out of the question for anyone who was not a baptised member of the institutional church. That position is no longer maintained, but the old saying has not been abandoned. It has been reinterpreted in an inclusive rather than an exclusive sense. Thus Maritain wrote: 'The saying "No salvation outside the Church" can only shock those who are ignorant of the soul of the Church. All it means to us is that there is no salvation outside the truth. Every man of good faith and good will, provided he doesn't sin against the light and doesn't refuse the grace offered him, belongs to the Soul of the Church.'[4] Here too the old saying about no salvation outside the church has been retained only by the expedient of redefining the church in that context to mean all those who respond to truth, whatever their links or lack of links with the church in the normal sense of the word.

For reasons of this kind I am not convinced that the move from an exclusive to an inclusive understanding of the uniqueness of Christ and of Christianity can be satisfactorily maintained. If it is true at all, it means that the general relation of Christianity to other faiths can be known on the basis of our knowledge of Christianity alone, quite apart from any knowledge of those other faiths themselves. There seems to me something badly amiss with an approach that involves such a prejudgment of the issue. If that is an implication of our traditional christology with its identification of Jesus and the Logos, are we not bound to say, so much the worse for our traditional christology? The difficulties which historical studies raised for christology may in the long run help to save us from even worse embarrassments in an age of religious studies.

Let me at this point recall words of Lord Hailsham that I used in the first lecture.[5] The passage I quoted ended like this.

> To think of the world as about 6,000 years old enables the facts of the New Testament to be regarded easily as a culmination (as it was presented in the first century) or relatively easily as the prelude to a climax (which it has been between the second and the twentieth). But when it has come to be believed that the human race has been present on the planet for millions of years, and may, for aught we know, continue to be present for an indefinite time in the future, the uniqueness of the Christian religion requires to be demonstrated in quite a different way.

He too regards the traditional understanding of uniqueness as in need of reassessment. But what prompts him to that view is not so much Christianity's changing relation to other faiths as the changing time scale within which the Christian understands himself to be set. His emphasis is an important and a helpful one. May not the narrowness of the geographical horizons, the shortness of the time scale and the nature of their imminent apocalyptic expectations all have contributed to the early Christians expressing what was rightly experienced as unique and world-transforming for them in terms of a more absolute and categorical uniqueness? And if that be so, may it not be incumbent upon us to re-express that uniqueness for our time in a more existential way, which will not involve any prejudgment about the status of other faiths? It was something along these lines that I was feeling after in the final section of my last lecture. I was trying to do justice to the indispensable character of the transforming power of Jesus and the incarnate Christ tradition for my apprehension of and response to God, but to do so in a way which left open the relation of that faith to other faiths. Does such an approach open up the way for a positive and genuinely theological view of Christianity, which can yet look on other religions as alternative ways of response to God?

If it does, it will certainly not be allowed to do so (and should not want to do so) without first being subjected to searching criticism. For the person I was criticizing a little while ago may well want to turn to the attack and object to me in some such terms as these. 'You accused me of being "charitable" in the bad sense of that word. But you are being "tolerant" in the bad sense of that word. You are "tolerant" in the sense of opting for anything that will avoid unpleasantness. You don't seem to care if there are conflicts of belief and that means you don't care about truth. If a Christian is committed to any conviction whatever, then he or she is committed to denying its contradictory. There is no escape from being polemical. If someone says the moon is made of green cheese, I may be tolerant of him; I can't be tolerant of his belief and regard it as another road to truth. Still more if Adolf Hitler or Charles Manson propounds a religious belief which calls for the extermination of Jews or of white bourgeois pigs, I cannot be tolerant of such beliefs. I must do all in my power not only to stop their being put into practice, but also to prevent their dissemination. In short, if all faiths are equally true, then all faiths are equally false. Concern for truth has gone out of the window and a disastrous loss of substance ensues.'

That challenge must be met. But my opponent has overplayed his hand (or, to be fair, I have made my opponent do so and have no right therefore to hold it against him!). I did not say that all religions were equally true. That would indeed be a silly thing to say. Some religions are poor (even demonic) intellectually, morally and spiritually. All that I am saying is that Christianity is not the only religion that has a *prima facie* claim to truth and spiritual profundity, and that any judgment on the relation of two such religions cannot legitimately be made on the basis of a knowledge of Christianity alone. It can only properly be done on the basis of a knowledge of both at comparable levels of understanding.

Whether that is a practicable enterprise is something to which I shall return in a moment. But first more needs to be said about the theoretical nature of what is being suggested. Three important considerations about the nature of religion need to be borne in mind.

1. The first concerns the nature of religious language. Of course when we affirm anything to be true we exclude the truth of its contradiction. And you cannot make a self-contradiction

meaningful by the simple expedient of dubbing it a 'paradox'. Nevertheless in the areas of personal and poetic discourse it is not always easy to know what does and what does not constitute a contradiction. The truth about human action, for example, seems to include aspects of freedom and determinism that we find hard to fit together without apparent contradiction. A poet may sometimes use two formally incompatible images in a single poem, not just for the fun of it but as the way that comes nearest to enabling him to communicate the reality he has apprehended.

Now it is with this sort of discourse that religious language belongs. Of course it includes many utterances of a comparatively straightforward factual kind. 'Jesus died on a cross' or 'Jesus said: "I and my Father are one"' are straightforward historical statements; their meaning is clear enough and, if we want to determine their truth or falsity, we must set about it by straightforward historical means. The evidence available may or may not prove sufficient for us to reach a firm conclusion, but the character of the statements and what would constitute their truth or falsity raise no special problems. But statements such as 'Jesus died for our sins' or 'I and my Father are one' are more distinctively religious utterances and are of a much more elusive character. The stress that I want to lay here on what has been called the logical oddity of religious language is no special pleading in support of a particular approach to the inter-religious debate. It is a stress that needs to be made all the time within Christian theology itself. We find ourselves forced to speak there, for example, both of God's eternity and of God's relation to time. This does not give us the right to affirm whatever we like however self-contradictory it may appear. We do not simply leave contradictory statements standing side by side as if it were a matter of indifference – or as if the paradox were paradoxically evidence in support of what we are affirming. But neither on the other hand do we immediately abandon one of our two apparently contradictory affirmations. We test them as carefully as we can, and if to abandon either would be to deny some aspect of our experience that we cannot deny with integrity, then (and only then) we are justified in holding on to both, provisionally at any rate, as the least inadequate expression of the truth available to us.

This characteristic of theological method applies also to the relation between different faiths. Perhaps the most basic difference between Western and Eastern religions is that between a personal and an impersonal understanding of God. Is this a case of direct incompatibility? What is striking is that already within each tradition are to be found important moves in the direction of the other. Thus within Christianity there is a profound mystical tradition which eschews personal language in its talk of God; and within Hinduism, there is the Bhakti tradition with its stress on personal divine grace. May it not be that the transcendent truth that we are seeking to express in talking of God demands these differing and formally contradictory expressions as complementary aspects of a single truth? That is not to claim that everything affirmed by every faith can be accommodated in a single all-embracing truth. Some conflicts and contradictions between faiths are genuine conflicts and contradictions. But it is to claim that some apparently contradictory claims may correspond to complementary truths about the one, ineffable God.

2. The other two general characteristics of religion I shall refer to much more briefly. I have been speaking about religious beliefs expressed in religious language. But religions are much more than sets of words and intellectual beliefs. To use an ugly phrase, they are 'encultured entities'. That is to say they are ways of articulating and practising a response to God in the particular situation of a people's life. Differing cultures may differ radically in world-view and in social patterns of life. In drastically different situations of that kind different words and different images may be required to effect basically the same purpose. Lord Hailsham's insistence on the difference between a first- and a twentieth-century outlook reveals the existence of this problem within Christianity itself. And such cultural divergences exist geographically as well as chronologically. We must be careful not to press this argument so far that it would imply that anything goes, that anything in any religion can be justified by the differing cultural conditions within which it is set. But we must press it far enough to ensure that we take proper cognizance of this additional complexity in any comparison of differing faiths.

3. The third consideration emerges even more clearly than the second from the general approach of these lectures. Relig-

ions are not static and unchanging; they are dynamic, changing entities. Being a Christian today is a very different (though not of course a totally different) thing from being a Christian in the fourth or fourteenth century. I have stressed how difficult (perhaps even mistaken) a process it is to try to isolate an unchanging 'essence' of Christianity. But even those who are well aware of that problem in relation to their own faith are in danger of forgetting it when it comes to other faiths with which they are less familiar. But the same is true of them also. Similar problems confront any attempt to isolate the 'essence' of Buddh-ism. So to the already existing difficulties of comparing faiths, we must add the further difficulty that what we would be engaged in is the comparison of two constantly changing entities.

If the task then is one of such complexity, can it be done at all? In some measure, at least, I believe it can. That is more a judg-ment of faith than one that can be adequately demonstrated, for we have barely begun the process of entering into one another's faiths at the depth of understanding that is called for. Yet there are indications that the kind of empathy required, the kind of passing-over into the faith of another, is not an impossibility. I have heard Muslim students say that the understanding of their own faith has been deepened by the writings of such a man as Kenneth Cragg. And Kenneth Cragg, for all his sympathetic interpretation of Islam, remains a profoundly and explicitly Christian writer. I see him therefore as a symbol of what may be achieved in the future, in a climate more generally encouraging to such mutual exploration of religions. Nor should it be thought that such a process requires a diminution of one's own faith. Indeed the very reverse has been claimed. Thus Simone Weil wrote: 'There are those who think they are capable of impartial-ity because they only have a vague religiosity which they can turn indifferently in any direction, whereas, on the contrary, we must have given all our attention, all our faith, all our love to a particular religion in order to think of any other religion with the high degree of attention, faith and love which is proper to it.'[6]

But my aim in this lecture is strictly limited. I am concerned with the implications for Christian theology of the general change in outlook that characterizes our age of religious studies. In my first lecture I described the task of the contemporary theologian as a critical re-evaluation of the Christian tradition we have received on the basis of the best knowledge available to us from all sources. And those sources include the insights we derive from a general study of religions. I was also insisting just now that religions are always changing entities. So if the impact of religious studies is to produce modifications in the form and content of Christian theology, it is merely contributing to a process that has been going on all through Christian history. It is much too early to say what those modifications will be. Certainly I do not myself begin to have either the knowledge or the experience of any other faith that would be required even for a preliminary evaluation of the changes that are likely to arise from closer interaction with the other great religions of the world. But there is one change that seems to arise inescapably from the mere fact of the existence of other religions as acknowledged forms of faith and of communion with God, quite apart from detailed knowledge of the particular contents of any one of them. That is a modification of the kind of absoluteness and uniqueness that we claim for Christ and the Christian faith. It is that therefore that I have sought to stress in these lectures.

Does that imply that we are taking the first step towards a full scale syncretism, towards a merging of all particular religions in one comprehensive world religion? I think not. Poetic imagery thrives on the concrete. If you try to say everything at once, you will end up by saying nothing at all with force or clarity. So too with the apprehension of God. We have begun to learn this truth in relation to differing styles of Christian belief. Catholic, Protestant, Orthodox, Pentecostal – each embodies distinctive ways of understanding, distinctive forms of response to God. Each also has shortcomings – elements of imbalance, and maybe also of sheer error. They ought not to coexist in complacent isolation; they need to share in a continuing process of mutual learning and correction. But neither ought they to seek for a single undifferentiated unity. For each has developed its own distinctive traditions and imagery out of which it lives. Merge these in a single synthesis, and there would be more loss than gain – not only in terms of practical life, but also in potential forms for the apprehension of the truth. The Ecumenical Movement has helped us to travel some way along this road. But we still have a good deal to learn about how to live in a pluralistic

Christian context, in a way that fully accepts other traditions than our own as an enrichment of humanity's knowledge of God while at the same time seeking mutual correction of those weaknesses that are a feature of every theological tradition.

But even though there is still scope for much more progress in this respect in the relations of Christians to one another, it is not too soon to begin asking whether it may not be along similar lines that we should be looking for a Christian theology in relation to other faiths. The vision I have in mind can be further illustrated by the way we already think of the relation of Christian thought to differing philosophies. Fundamental to the story of early Christianity is the account of how in the first centuries of our era it came into relation with the platonism of the time. The outcome was not a straightforward syncretism, but it was a platonic or platonized form of Christian belief, one which incorporated distinctive insights of platonism and interpreted its own beliefs from a recognizably platonic angle. Now we are inclined to think of that story as an example of the relation of Christianity and philosophy, and to see that as something quite distinct from the relation between Christianity and other faiths. But the distinction between the two is not absolute. The platonism of the early Christian world was a strongly religious philosophy. It was not simply a vehicle through which an already well developed Christian faith found appropriate expression. It inhibited the development of some aspects of early Christianity, helped others to grow and find more adequate expression, and also itself contributed constructively both to the form and the content of Christian believing in the Hellenistic world. May we perhaps look forward in the long run to the emergence of distinctively Buddhistic and Islamic forms of Christian theology? By those terms I envisage forms of Christian theology in which insights central to Buddhism and Islam – and only fully accessible and expressed within those faiths – will have been allowed to mould and modify Christian belief in a way which will illuminate and deepen aspects of belief implied but only imperfectly realized in other forms of Christian theology. Such a vision does not, of course, rule out critical judgments in relation to other faiths, any more than it does in relation to other forms of Christian faith in an ecumenical dialogue, or should do in relation to one's own faith. What it would do would be to rule out all claims to an exclusive truth or an exhaustive apprehension of God in one's own tradition.

What are the implications of such an approach for the practical ministry of the Christian church in which most of you are or will be engaged and with which every Christian theologian should be concerned? That, I suspect, will vary according to the situation in which your ministry is set. In some cases it may weaken the immediate impact of the gospel as traditionally preached. For we would not be able to speak of it as the truth for all peoples and for all times. But I do not believe it would diminish one iota of its real spiritual message. For we would still be able to speak of the Christian gospel as the primary form in which the truth of God has come to us in our culture; we would still be able to speak of it as one of such profound spiritual worth that it ought to be shared with other people throughout the globe. And some at least of those who hear it so presented may be freer to respond, because they will no longer be offended (justifiably offended) by the feeling that what may be a truth apprehended by the preacher is being presented to them as the truth without qualification. And this will be achieved without that gospel being robbed of its particularity, its history, its images – all those things that give it vitality – and being turned into some all-embracing and all-deadening generality.

I said at the outset that the task of the theologian was to point a possible way forward for the church. I do not expect the way that I have been depicting to meet with universal acceptance. But I offer it in the hope that when tested it may prove to combine the two essential concomitants of any rightful way – namely life and truth.

PART II

4

The Patristic Appeal to Tradition

We know about the gospel of Jesus because down the ages people have talked about him, written about him, lived particular kinds of lives because of him. In some sense the first disciples could be said to have known that gospel directly. Thus the author of I John speaks of that 'which we have heard, which we have seen with our eyes, which we have looked upon and touched with our hands, concerning the word of life' (I John 1.1). Whether or not the author was himself an eye-witness, it can certainly be said of that awkwardly-phrased opening of the epistle that (in the words of a recent commentator) 'it helps to bind the writer to those who stand behind him, those who literally saw Jesus and witnessed the original events of the life-giving Gospel'.[1] Somewhere at the back of it all there were those of whom it could be said (as Jesus had said of Thomas) that they had seen and believed – though even then, as the gospels frequently remind us, it was only too easily possible to see and not to see.

But even in the apostolic age, even before the writing of the First Epistle of John, such a direct knowledge of gospel origins belonged only to a very small minority of Christians. For the great majority such knowledge was a transmitted knowledge. Paul describes the process of transmission very clearly in I Cor. 15.3: 'I delivered to you as of first importance what I also received, that Christ died for our sins in accordance with the scriptures.' The compound words that he uses – παραδίδωμι and παραλαμβάνω, translated as 'delivered' and 'received', with the repeated prefix 'para' signifying movement from beside one person or place and arrival alongside another – vividly depict a chain of transmitted knowledge. And the content of what was so transmitted was not bare facts but a way of understanding those facts, not just what was seen but what was seen and believed, not simply that Jesus died but that Christ died for our sins according to the scriptures.

The writing of the New Testament was, in part at least, a codification in more permanent form of that which was being transmitted in this way. But it did not straightaway alter the underlying picture in terms of which that process of transmission was envisaged. Thus Papias, bishop of Hierapolis in Asia Minor about AD 135 speaks of himself as having taken delight in 'those who recall the commandments given by the Lord to faith, and reaching us from the truth itself'. He then goes on:

> And if anyone chanced to come who had actually been a follower of the elders, I would enquire about the discourses of the elders – what Andrew, Peter, Philip, Thomas, James, John, Matthew or any other of the Lord's disciples had said; or what Aristion and John the elder, disciples of the Lord, say. For I did not think that the contents of books would profit me as much as the utterances of a living and abiding voice.[2]

Papias certainly knew some of our gospels. For it is from him that we have those first tantalizing references to Mark being the interpreter of Peter and of Matthew compiling the oracles in Hebrew (or Aramaic). Nevertheless his basic picture of the transmission of the faith is of a chain of oral tradition stretching back to the living voice of Jesus, who himself was, or rather is, the truth.

But it was inevitable that with the passage of time and the geographical expansion of the church the balance would have to change. We catch a glimpse of that process just beginning in the roughly contemporary epistle of Polycarp to the Philippians. In it he speaks of

> the blessed and glorious Paul, who when he was among you in the presence of the men of that time taught accurately and stedfastly the word of truth, and also when he was absent wrote letters to you, from the study of which you will be able to build yourselves up in the faith you have been given.[3]

The way in which Polycarp expresses himself suggests that the pattern of oral transmission is still for him the archetypal form of the transmission of the faith. But the content of what he has to say clearly reveals the greater practical utility of the written form of that message.

By the closing years of the second century, although formal canonization of the New Testament as we now have it was still two centuries away, there was in practice a more or less fixed set of authoritative writings roughly corresponding to our New Testament. And the shifting balance of emphasis of which I have been speaking has been taken a stage further. The same underlying conception with an increased emphasis on the written word is clearly evident in the work of Irenaeus, Bishop of Lyons towards the end of the second century. In his book entitled 'Against the Heresies' he describes it in this way:

> The Lord of all gave to his apostles the power of the gospel, and by them we also have learned the truth ... For we learned the plan of our salvation from no others than from those through whom the gospel came to us. They first preached it abroad, and then later by the will of God handed it down to us in scriptures, to be the foundation and pillar of our faith.[4]

Although he dubs them 'the foundation and pillar of our faith', Irenaeus does not regard the scriptures as absolutely essential. What has been conveyed to the majority of Christians by the apostolic writings has been conveyed to some barbarian tribes, who are ignorant of the necessary languages, by oral transmission alone. And it has been conveyed to them in so firm a form that they would prove just as resistant to perversions of the gospel as those with access to the written tradition.

But Irenaeus and those who thought like him were not alone in viewing the transmission of the gospel in these terms. There was a large variety of Gnostic sects giving very different accounts of the content of Christian truth but very similar accounts of its transmission. The Ophites, for example, traced their teaching back to Jesus through James, the Lord's brother, and the followers of Basilides did the same through Matthias, the apostle who replaced Judas. Thus by diverse routes each Gnostic sect could claim to derive its peculiar tenets from the living and abiding voice of Jesus, that is of the truth itself.

How then was true tradition to be distinguished from false? By appeal to scripture as containing the most clearly fixed and reliable form of the tradition? Not simply by appeal to scripture, for many of the Gnostics also appealed to scripture and with the help of allegorical interpretation claimed to be able to show that it supported their own position. Then, by scripture interpreted in a sensible and reasonable manner? So Irenaeus argued and supported his claim with a splendid simile. This is how he contrasts his interpretation of scripture with that of his opponents.

> Their manner of acting is just as if, when a beautiful image of a king had been constructed out of precious jewels by some skilful artist, someone else were to take that likeness of a man to pieces, rearrange the gems and fit them together again into the form of a dog or a fox – and that but poorly executed; and were then to maintain that *that* was the beautiful image of the king the skilful artist had constructed ... and thereby deceive the ignorant, who had no conception what the form of a king was like, into believing that the wretched likeness of the fox was in fact the beautiful image of the king. That is just what these people do. By drawing the words, expressions and parables to be found in the different parts of scripture violently out of their context, they patch together old wives' tales and endeavour by that means to adapt the oracles of God to their baseless fictions.[5]

Certainly some extravagancies of interpretation could be ruled out in that way. But Irenaeus could not present himself straightforwardly as advocate of a purely literal interpretation of scripture. That course could only give rise to crudely anthropomorphic ideas about God which he was as anxious as any one to rule out. And the history of biblical scholarship ever since reinforces the conviction that scripture does not bear its meaning unmistakably upon its surface. Even if the ignorant and unstable are guilty of twisting the scriptures to their own destruction, as the author of II Peter asserts, one has also to admit with him that Paul (and other scriptural writers) have given them the opportunity of doing so by writing some things that are hard to understand (II Peter 3.15–16).

So scripture was unable to function as final arbiter of what was and what was not true tradition. Scripture and tradition were too closely bound together as interlocking parts of a single whole. For example, the vital question about the way in which scripture ought to be interpreted (which has to be settled before scripture can be used to discriminate between true and false tradition) was itself a feature of the tradition. Thus there is no clear starting-point in one which does not already involve the other. Indeed throughout the subsequent history of the church scripture and tradition have belonged together rather like some married couple who find it hard to live happily together but impossible to live at all apart.

If appeal to scripture then was unable to settle the issue, where else was it possible to turn in trying to distinguish true tradition from false? Since most Gnostic traditions were by definition esoteric traditions, handed down with great secrecy, any form of historical check was automatically excluded. But precisely there lay the pointer to the principal line of answer adopted by Irenaeus and the main body of the church. While the Gnostic tradition was a private and secret one, the church tradition was a public and open one. And therein lay the guarantee of its authenticity. 'It was there, in the Church', declares Irenaeus using another vivid simile 'that the apostles, like a rich man making a deposit, fully bestowed everything that belongs to the truth.'[6] 'Even if', he insists, pressing the point home against his opponents, 'the apostles had known of hidden mysteries, which they taught to the perfect secretly and apart from others, they would have handed them down especially to those to whom they were entrusting the churches themselves.'[7] In other words on the issue of tradition, it is bishops and not theological professors who count.

However much we may agree with that order of priority, we should not think of it as a self-evident truth to a Christian of Irenaeus' day. Religion is sacred and one ought not to cast pearls before swine. To many it seemed only natural that the deepest religious truths should have been handed down secretly to that restricted few 'to whom it has been given to know the secrets of the kingdom of heaven' (Matt. 13.11). Certainly Irenaeus' contemporary, Clement of Alexandria, who remained fully within the main body of the church, had an understanding of the way in which tradition was handed down that was much closer to that of the Gnostics than to that held by Irenaeus.

But there is something of even greater importance that needs to be acknowledged by those whose fundamental sympathies are with Irenaeus (as I believe they should be). Positions worked out in a polemical situation are always liable to be overstated. That certainly happens with Irenaeus. In making his claim against the Gnostics that the church tradition is the one truly derived from the teaching of the apostles, he claims that it has come down unchanged from their time. And in making his other claim against the Gnostics that the church's tradition is a public tradition handed on by the official leaders of the church, he claims that it has come down through an exact episcopal succession at Rome from the time when Peter and Paul ministered there. The early second century is a period for which our knowledge about the church is very scanty. But of these two things we can be reasonably certain. What Irenaeus believed was different in many ways from what the first apostles believed (if indeed we are justified in speaking of a common belief of the apostles as a group in the first place). And the pattern of ministry at Rome from the time of the founding of the church there to Irenaeus' day was far more variable than he imagined it to have been. His main point against the Gnostics may have been right, but he made it in far too rigid a form. And by doing so he bequeathed to the church a disastrous legacy from which it has not yet wholly freed itself – a legacy of the two great fictions of an unchanging doctrine and an unbroken succession of bishops from the time of the apostles.

But this sense of an unchanging tradition was to become even stronger and more rigid in the years that followed. Irenaeus spoke of the content of the tradition as 'the rule of truth'. It did not take the form of a specific creed; it did not involve any fixed form of words. It followed a more or less fixed pattern, but Irenaeus felt quite free to put it in his own words, as the purpose of the moment might require. But the church did not allow the content of the tradition to remain in that flexible form. Ensuing centuries saw wide varieties of interpretation develop, all of which could plausibly claim to fall within the framework of the same 'rule of truth' with which Irenaeus had worked. Both Arius and Athanasius could and did make equally genuine and equally plausible claims to be continuators of the old tradition. In spite of the great difference between them, it was possible for both their claims to be substantially true in view of the variegated nature of that earlier tradition. But the church felt bound to make a judgment one way or the other between them. And the process of doing so involved defining the tradition with an increasing degree of precision. One way in which it did so was by promulgation of the carefully constructed creed of Nicaea.

It is important to recognize that something happened there which was new both in principle and in specific detail. The content of the doctrinal tradition was defined with an untraditional exactitude; and the key phrase in so defining it was the untraditional word, *homoousios*. Unless that fact is firmly grasped, one is unlikely to assess aright the complex story of the reaction to Nicaea in the years after the Council and of the confusing array of creeds and counter-creeds through which that reaction expressed itself. The ultimate ineffectiveness of that movement and its search for alternatives to Nicaea did much to enhance the prestige of the Council. What that meant for the concept of tradition becomes clear a century later in the arguments and the attitudes to be found in the course of the bitter Nestorian controversy in the early years of the fifth century.

The substance of that debate concerned how the human and the divine natures of Christ were to be understood. Were they to be thought of as distinct to ensure that each was affirmed in its full integrity or were they to be thought of in an integrated way to ensure that it was one Christ and a real union of human and divine that was being affirmed? I am not concerned here with the substance of that debate. What is of interest in the context of the present discussion is the relation of both parties to the earlier faith of the church. As I see it, both parties to the debate stood in the same relation to the faith promulgated at the Council of Nicaea that the two parties in the Arian controversy had stood to the earlier tradition of the church, exemplified by Irenaeus' 'rule of truth'. Each side could and did claim to be sincere continuators of Nicaea. They were reluctant to admit that a genuinely new problem had arisen. Both sides (Cyril of Alexandria, in particular) claimed that their teaching was nothing more than an interpretation – the only possible interpretation – of Nicaea. Indeed they went further than that. Not only was it the only possible interpretation of Nicaea, it had been explicitly taught or clearly adumbrated by all the great figures of the past. Thus the protagonists on each side of the debate, Antiochenes and Alexandrians alike, prepared their rival dossiers of texts to show how men like Ignatius, Irenaeus, Hippolytus and

Methodius had favoured their particular dyophysite or mono-physite view as the case might be.

There were various ways in which that task was undertaken. Most economically it could be done by the age-old act of judicious selection. If that proved insufficient, it was always possible to resort to minor modifications of the texts concerned. If, for example, the form of the doxology in some early writers ('Glory be to the Father through the Son and through the Holy Spirit') seemed to favour a subordinate status of the Second and Third Persons of the Trinity, change of the link words from 'through' to 'and' would turn it into support for a coequal Trinity. It was not too hard to convince oneself that such changes were really recorrections of texts which had been adulterated by one's opponents in the first place. And if even that was not sufficient, one could always write one's own texts and ascribe them to an earlier age. So the later patristic period gives rise to a whole collection of pseudonymous writings, such as the longer recension of interpolated letters of Ignatius, the writings of pseudo-Justin and, most famously of all, the great corpus of writings of late fifth-century origin ascribed to Dionysius the Areopagite, the first-century convert of Paul's preaching at Athens. All these pseudonymous writings were designed to present what were really new insights and new convictions arising out of new problems of a later age as if they were the beliefs and convictions of earlier generations of Christians. In other words if you are sufficiently convinced that the tradition is fixed, you can easily prove your point by 'fixing' the tradition. And that was so effectively done that only the rise of historical critical method about a thousand years later was able to unscramble it – and perhaps has not fully done so even yet.

I have been speaking so far about the teaching or doctrinal tradition. But I said at the beginning that our knowledge of the gospel today was due not only to the fact that down the ages men and women have talked about it and written about it, but also that they have lived particular kinds of life because of it. Practice as well as teaching is a way of handing on the faith, and since faith is concerned with how people live as much as with what they say, non-verbal methods of communication are also of importance.

Christians do many things, including things of significance for their faith, for which no scriptural authority is to be found. The point is made explicitly by Tertullian at the very beginning of the third century. In arguing that the wearing of a laurel chaplet, as sometimes required of a soldier, is a pagan custom incompatible with loyalty to Christ, Tertullian admits that he cannot provide scriptural authority for his position, but is quite unabashed by the admission. The refusal of the chaplet is, he says, an observed custom and 'the very title "observed custom" is its own defence and is supported by the authority of established usage'.[8] The argument is so sweeping, that it is hard to treat it as other than characteristic Tertullianic exaggeration. Any scruples about so treating it are soon overcome, when we find Tertullian in another work written about the same time arguing precisely the opposite point. The work is entitled 'On the Veiling of Virgins' and in it Tertullian declares that it is 'from ignorance or simplicity that custom finds its beginning; it is then established into usage and so maintained against the truth. But Christ called himself Truth, not custom'.[9] It is clear that in practice customs, like traditions, call for discrimination.

When writing in defence of custom Tertullian goes on to list a range of Christian practices that he regards as customs fully established and agreed, despite the absence of written authorization for them. They are drawn mainly from liturgical practice. The performing of baptism in the presence of the congregation, including an act of renunciation of the devil and triple immersion; the celebration of the eucharist before dawn and its reception only from the hand of the president; eucharistic offerings for the dead on the anniversary of their death and a reverential attitude towards the consecrated elements; the exclusion of fasting and kneeling for worship on the Lord's day and during the Easter season; and finally the use of the sign of the cross in connection with many actions of daily life.[10]

Such liturgical traditions cannot really be separated from the teaching tradition. For if they are of any importance in the practice of piety, they may often prove more effective purveyors of religious conviction and religious attitudes than words. Their tendency is likely to be in a conservative direction. And that natural tendency is reinforced in the patristic age by a feature of the picture closely parallel to that which I have emphasized in relation to the doctrinal tradition. Many customs were wrongly believed to be much earlier in origin than they really were, to go back indeed to apostolic times. And this erroneous belief was once again reinforced by pseudonymous writings. Just as later legend ascribed each clause of the Apostles' Creed to individual apostles, so the author of the Apostolic Constitutions, probably a fourth-century Syrian of Arian sympathies, could ascribe to the apostles the most detailed record of the legislative and liturgical practices that he desired to see in the life of the church. And as late as the eighteenth century an erudite man like William Whiston (who was Newton's successor as professor of mathematics at Cambridge and shared Newton's interest in religious questions) could still be taken in by the deception and make that work the main plank in his own programme for what he called Primitive Christianity Revived in the belief that it was a genuine product of the first century.

Many factors combined to give to tradition the extremely important place and the particular form that it took in the thought of the Fathers. As I said at the very beginning, if the gospel is a gospel about Jesus Christ some form of tradition is required for us to know about it at all. And if the gospel gives to Christ the unique significance for revelation and redemption that Christianity has always ascribed to him, then the desire for accurate and precise tradition will be greatly reinforced. But this specifically Christian concern was further influenced in the particular shape that it took by more general attitudes to ancient tradition in the Hellenistic world as a whole. It was a characteristic of both religious and philosophical attitudes to ascribe an almost unqualified authority to some traditional source or figure in the past. For Plotinus the neoplatonist, for example, it would seem that it was impossible ever to disagree with Plato.[11] Where he wanted to say things that were different from what Plato had said, he had to convince himself that they were really the proper interpretation of what Plato had meant. All these more general considerations lay at the back of the historical development that I have been describing.

In practice the Fathers were often more original than they were prepared to admit even to themselves. New ideas were made to masquerade as old ones. The form in which they understood and presented their own work did not always do justice to the creativity that marks the thought of the best of them. Tradition remains of great importance for us, not only as the irreplaceable link with the Christian past but also as something to which we may need to appeal in debate with eccentric interpretations claiming the authority of the Spirit and of immediate experience. But such an appeal cannot play as large a role with us as it did with the Fathers nor can it play its role in the same way as it did for them. The *Zeitgeist* within which we live is in this respect almost as different as it could be from theirs. Our sense of the historical relativity both of ideas and of customs precludes us from giving to any ancient authority the absolute status that it seemed natural to them to do. If we are to be true to ourselves, we will have to approach all our traditional authorities (including the Fathers themselves) in a critical and questioning spirit that they would never have allowed themselves to employ in relation to their revered predecessors in the faith. In this respect we have to be very different from them.

What would such a difference of approach involve in practice? Let me try to answer that question briefly from my own experience. The earlier part of my career as a theologian was spent in studying and teaching the early history of Christian doctrine. My approach to that early patristic tradition, including the creeds, was the same as that of any serious biblical scholar to the biblical texts. One treated them as the writings of fallible human beings seeking as best they could to record, to interpret and to make sense of their experience in terms of the knowledge and culture of their day. In the case of the Fathers that involved understanding the Bible very differently from the way in which it is understood by Christians today and working out their convictions in terms of a philosophy very different from our own. How could such an approach, I found myself reflecting, however faithfully fulfilled, be thought to provide an unchanging framework of truth for all time? To conceive that it could was not so much an expression of faithfulness to God and to his revelation; it was more like a refusal to take history seriously, more like making an idol out of particular forms of words. Just as the nineteenth century found itself committed to the painful but necessary task of 'biblical criticism', so it seemed to me was our age committed to the equally necessary but equally painful task of 'doctrinal' or 'credal criticism'.[12] As the work of the biblical critic at its best can make the Bible live more truly for us, not in spite of but through what seems at first to be the disturbing, even threatening, work of criticism, so in the long run may the work of the doctrinal or credal critic prove to do. Ray Hart has expressed the theme that I am seeking to convey with the aid of a vigorous image worthy to be set alongside that of Irenaeus which I cited earlier in this lecture: 'Tradition', he wrote, 'must be dismantled to see what it mediates, what it handed around and hands on. Mediating only in dissolution, tradition furnishes debris for building up the structure to house what it could not hold against the flood of time.'[13] In other words tradition has to acknowledge that basic law of Christian living that the one who would save his life loses it while the one who loses his life gains it. So the Christian has to live in a dialectical situation between critical attention to the ancient tradition and equally critical attention to what makes sense for our life in the world today.

Such a process involves an element of risk. But risk is endemic to the life of the gospel. We may go a-whoring after the fads of modernity and be seduced into distorting the truth we have received. But that need not be the outcome. Indeed if we do our task as well as the Fathers did theirs it may turn out that we shall find a point of meeting even in the midst of a great difference. I said just now that the best of them were in fact more genuinely original and creative than their conception of what was involved in loyalty to tradition allowed them to admit. Perhaps if we pursue our task faithfully, we may turn out in the end to have been more traditional than the critical temper of our times would allow us to expect. I do not say that will happen. But of one thing I am sure. It has more chance of happening that way than if we try to be traditional in precisely the way that they tried to be traditional. For to follow that road in our world today would be to follow a road leading to sterility and death.

5

In What Sense is Christianity a 'Historical' Religion?

'It belongs to the specific character of Christianity that it is an historical religion' wrote C. H. Dodd and a recent article about him begins by quoting those words as expressing a central motif in every book he wrote.[1] 'Christianity, like its Jewish parent, is an historical religion' are also the opening words of John Drury's book *Tradition and Design in Luke's Gospel*.[2] Yet Dodd and Drury are far from holding identical views about the relation of Christianity to history. What does this much quoted phrase 'a historical religion' imply and why is the thing implied felt to be so vital to the Christian faith? It is those two questions that I want to explore – the meaning of the phrase and the reasons for regarding it as indicating something of crucial importance to the very existence of Christianity.

1. Every theologian, however inadequate his knowledge of German, is aware of the distinction between the two words *historisch* and *geschichtlich* and the wealth of theological significance attaching thereto. The ambiguity of the English word 'historical' is less frequently discussed but it certainly exists. Let me give a hypothetical example. The Sex Discrimination Act has led even Oxford colleges to consider whether they should admit women. In the course of a discussion of the question on the governing body of such a college, one can envisage someone saying 'we must remember that the college is a historical entity'. The remark might be a contribution on either side of the debate. It might mean either: 'The college was founded 450 years ago with a particular form and constitution that excluded women; we are not therefore free to do whatever we like with it; we are bound by its historical character and must remain faithful

to that' or alternatively it might mean 'a college is something that exists through time; by gradual process of adaptation in the course of its history it has changed in innumerable ways from the kind of institution it originally was; it is its existence as a historical entity prepared to adapt itself to changing circumstance that ensures its continuing life and vitality, and for that reason it behoves us to make this change now'. The conflicting implications of calling something 'historical' suggested by that illustration do not need much modification in order to apply them to the Christian church; the specific issue of the admission of women would not need to be changed.

So let me give two specific examples from theological writers to show the range of meaning the term may have there. Gordon Kaufman objects to a mythical interpretation of the fall and declares: 'The fall was ... an actual historical event – though not one that happened in a moment to some solitary couple in paradise. It was an event of many generations' duration that happened to the species *homo sapiens* in its historical development. ... The Christian faith is eminently historical not only because it sees man's being as radically immersed in history, but because it understands that the evil from which man must be saved is a diseasedness and contamination of this historical process and historical being, which man himself has effected through his historical action.'[3] Since we live in an evolutionary world, everything that is the case about the human race and about the world in which we live has become what it is by a gradual, historical process. The word is used by Kaufman with so broad a connotation that it is difficult to see how any faith – indeed how anything at all – could avoid meriting the definition 'historical'. At the other extreme take this quotation from Eric Mascall's inaugural lecture as Professor of Historical Theology at King's College, London: 'It has often been emphasized that Christianity is historical in a sense in which no other religion is, for it stands or falls by certain events which are alleged to have taken place during a particular period of forty-eight hours in Palestine nearly two thousand years ago.' Mascall also quotes Dom Gregory Dix as having said that Christianity 'is the only fully historical religion. It is the only religion which actually depends entirely upon history ...'.[4]

Professor Mascall expresses himself with his usual clarity and forthrightness. But the general position that he propounds so vigorously is the sort of position that is usually intended by those who stress the distinctively and essentially historical character of the Christian faith. But before going on to analyse the grounds for such a claim, I want first (as would seem appropriate) to consider it historically – how and when did this kind of assertion originate – and secondly to distinguish various forms in which the claim might reasonably be put.

(*a*) Proponents of the position I am concerned with might want to object that since they are describing something that is characteristic of Christianity as such, it has no separate history. The history of the idea would be the history of Christianity itself. It has been, so they might argue, a conscious feature of Christian theology from the earliest days when in the first and second centuries Christianity distinguished itself from Gnostic perversions. Their objection has some force. There are important links between their position and the stance of second-century anti-Gnostic Christian writers. Nevertheless those links fall well short of full identity. Modern developments of historical method and consequent changes in historical understanding mean that there is bound to be a distinctively modern way of expressing – and still more of feeling – the conviction.

I can best illustrate the kind of difference involved by reference to two writers who draw attention to important changes in the understanding of such a phrase as 'historical Christianity' in the course of the nineteenth century. Martin Kähler insists that for him 'Christianity ... is *the* historical religion because it originates from a history absolutely normative, from historical revelation'. He is concerned to stress the point in that way in order to distinguish his own position from that of many of his theological contemporaries, for whom ' "historical Christianity" means that historical Christianity which has evolved from century to century'.[5] J. M. Creed, the other writer to whom I want to refer, describes a similar phenomenon not in terms of a changed understanding of the same phrase but rather in terms of a change in terminology. 'In the nineteenth century,' he writes, 'it became less usual than it had been to speak of Christianity as "Revealed Religion" and commoner to speak of it as "a historical religion" or "the Historic Faith".'[6] Kähler saw the tendency of which he disapproved so strongly as due to a regrettable tendency to 'think that the Reformers' stand upon the Bible was only a relic from the past'. Creed, who was more sympathetic to the trend he was describing, sees it as arising out of the shift from a primarily dogmatic to a primarily historical treatment of the Bible. He did not see the change involved as constituting a total reversal of earlier attitudes. He puts the point like this: 'It is not to be overlooked that these two views of Christianity, which we may distinguish from each other by the phrases "The Revealed Religion" and "The Historic Faith", have a factor in common which is essential to each: in the one case as in the other the Christian religion includes – nay it rests upon – certain historical figures and certain historical events which form a part of the general history of mankind. But the relation of Christianity to the general history of mankind is very different, according as Christianity is "The Revealed Religion" or "The Historic Faith".'[7] Creed's language matches that of Mascall and Dix – 'stands or falls by'; 'depends entirely upon'; 'rests upon'. Moreover he would agree that this is a characteristic of Christianity at all times. It is not the new thing that gives rise to the shift in terminology bringing to the fore the 'historical' character of Christianity. That was linked rather with a new insistence that the church was 'not so much the depository and guardian of a Revelation committed to it, as the continuous historical embodiment of the religion itself'.[8] But that new emphasis was bound to affect the way in which the old, continuing insistence on the foundation character of certain particular events was apprehended. In the earlier synthesis the truth of the text and of the history coincided. Part of the novelty of the nineteenth-century situation was that that synthesis had fallen apart, a choice had had to be made between them and that choice, according to Creed, had fallen on the side of history. Thus while stress on the importance of the happening was not wholly new, it did take on a different flavour in its new situation of greater separation from its old companion, the divinely guaranteed text. Moreover that stress had to live with a new companion, the other aspect of Christianity's historicality, namely the church as continuous historical embodiment of the faith and the two were uneasy bedfellows.

(*b*) This leads me on therefore to the further issue. In what form can the claim that Christianity 'rests upon certain historical figures and certain historical events' be put, once it has been transposed into its new context with a balancing emphasis on continuing historical embodiment rather than being seen as part of a wholly *sui generis* once-for-all revelation? Clearly it cannot take the form of making essential the historical existence of all the people who figure on the pages of the Bible or the historical factuality of all the events recorded there. The patent impossibility of making such a claim was one important factor that helped to give rise to the general change of attitude that I have been describing. Even the older approach had not been absolutely wedded to such a position. Allegorical exegesis had left a way open for combining a view of Christianity as a faith wholly and infallibly revealed in scripture with a denial of the historicity of some at first sight apparently historical features of it. But whatever might have been the case in the past, any such claim in the nineteenth or twentieth century was wholly out of the question. What then were or are these indispensable historical figures and historical events? Let me sketch two possible positions:

(*i*) It might be claimed that what is essential is the historical factuality of the main outline events of salvation-history. This position was one often put forward when I first read theology, as a reassurance to those of us who were having to come to terms for the first time with a critical approach to scripture and relate it to our Christian faith. As an example I quote some words of Gabriel Hebert. 'We are justified', he wrote, 'in distinguishing the main outline of the history and its cardinal events from episodes such as would never be mentioned in any summary of the history; such episodes as the history of Absalom's rebellion, or of the conversion of the Ethiopian eunuch in Acts 8. These are authentic historical narratives, but such that if they were legendary, or if the events had not been recorded, the main course of the history would scarcely be affected. But if the Exodus story were not in substance true, the faith of Israel about its own vocation would be grounded on a falsehood.'[9]

I am not for the moment concerned with the logic of Hebert's position – I shall be coming to that later – but simply with getting clear what that position is. For him the historical figures and historical events on which Christian faith rests are those that figure in the main outline of that history in which God has worked his Purpose[10] of salvation. This provides some degree of precision as to what is the history on which Christianity depends, but inevitably that degree is strictly limited. There is no agreed account of what does or does not belong to the outline of that history – it would hardly, for example, be taken to include all the incidents referred to in the outline given in Stephen's speech in Acts 7, some of which are not even recorded in the Old Testament. Or again what constitutes the Exodus story being 'in substance true'? Would it have to include a miraculous crossing of the Red Sea and the drowning of the Egyptians? What proportion of the ancestors of the later people of Israel would have to have been involved? But for the moment let us be content simply to note these difficulties, without trying to decide whether or not they are fatal to the theory as a whole.

(*ii*) More frequently the claim is likely to be restricted to Jesus. Mascall indeed restricts it to 'a particular period of forty-eight hours'. Here too there are bound to be difficulties in determining just how much is being insisted on. Another recent writer speaks, for example, of 'the very small area of fact which is absolutely necessary as a basis for faith'.[11] But what exactly is that very small area? In the same paragraph he refers to it as 'the fact of Jesus Christ'. Presumably more is meant than the bare fact that there existed someone with the name Joshua-bar-Miriam; something at least to the effect that the records of his character and teaching are (to use Hebert's phrase) 'in substance true'. But here there are special problems indicated by our need to use the plural word 'records'. Is there a coherent character and teaching of all four gospels which could be 'in substance true' of a single historical individual? Perhaps, but certainly only if 'in substance' is given a pretty broad definition.

Furthermore most accounts that see Christianity as dependent on the historical figure of Jesus and historical events concerning him are likely to include the resurrection among those historical events. If so, the problem of miracle and its relation to history remains a major issue which is bound to complicate the way in which Christianity's dependence on history is to be understood and defended.

2. The question of deciding how much, if any, of the historical factuality desiderated by such theories can be established by normal historical means (whatever exactly they may be!) is an

immensely complex one. Work related to it goes on all the time in the regular course of that historical study of the Bible which looms so large in undergraduate study of theology, at any rate in Oxford. But that is not my concern here. I want to pursue a different question – you might call it a prior question but then that might be prejudging a number of issues. The question I want to ask is this: Why should this dependence on history be regarded as indispensable to Christian faith?

I am not sure how far it is possible to tackle so fundamental a question, but I think the attempt is worth making. Certainly the hypothetical opponent whose basic stance I am calling into question is likely to challenge the validity of the question altogether. I can imagine his reacting something like this: 'Your question makes no sense. You might as well ask why having four legs or chewing the cud is indispensable to the being of a cow; they are simply part of the definition of what it is to be a cow. They are necessary truths, true by definition. So Christianity simply is a religion that depends on these historical events as its necessary (though not sufficient) ground. Without them Christianity would simply cease to be Christianity. You yourself have had to admit this in effect in what you said about the anti-Gnostic writers and the continuity between Christianity understood as "Revealed Religion" and "Historic Faith". Your admissions were highly damaging to the thrust of your argument. You couldn't escape making them, but you've simply gone on trying to evade their force. You would do much better now to admit that for good or ill that is the nature of Christianity and give up asking your sophisticated but nonetheless stupid questions.' Part of me sympathizes with the objector, is tempted to tear up the paper I am in process of writing and join (or rejoin) the ranks of the simple believers, the biblical theologians or some such grouping. But the part is less than half; so (for good or ill) the paper survives and will go on.

When the objector says that without this historical dependence Christianity would simply cease to be Christianity, how does he know? Let us grant that in one form or another it has been a feature of Christianity throughout its history. That does not by itself prove his point. Other things have characterized Christianity for the greater part of its history without our being led thereby to regard them as indispensable or unalterable – the absolute reliability of the sacred text, God's special creation of man, a negative attitude to other religions, even the refusal of ordination to women. One needs to be able to say more than that it has always been a feature of Christianity; one needs to be able to say that it belongs to the essence of Christianity. How is such a claim to be made? Can it be supported by argument or is it something one either sees to be so – or fails to see, as the case may be?

It is not enough to say that it is a feature of the creed. The creed certainly includes historical statements. The Virgin Birth is one example. Yet many even of those who hold strongly to that belief would acknowledge the full Christian status of those who do not and would not insist on its historicity as essential to Christian faith. So if that historically very important example of a historical claim, enshrined in the Apostles' Creed and a focal point of much profound spiritual devotion, can be regarded as not essential, can we be sure (simply on the ground of there being a number of examples of historical statements in the creed) that the principle of historical dependence as such is absolutely essential?

The difficulty of finding appropriate arguments here is that they will have to make some sort of assumption about what is essential, and this is itself a major part of our problem. There is, for example, a difference between saying that what is essential is faith in Jesus as the Christ and describing it as faith in God through Jesus Christ. The former gives to the historical event a more firmly entrenched position than the latter. Thus Brunner, for example, is one of those who asserts that 'the very existence of the Christian religion depends on vital connection with an "accidental" fact of history' and that 'it is precisely this connection with a "brute fact" which is the distinguishing mark of the Christian religion.'[12] But for him this is something which the man of faith simply sees and the Messianic claim is at the heart of it. 'It may sound fine', he writes, 'to say: "Faith has no interest at all in these facts"; but this lofty indifference is forbidden to us by faith. It is of importance to see that this "circle", which is so indistinct that many historians cannot "see" it at all, should really exist. We do not build our faith upon it, but as believers who also desire to look at the historical aspect of the question, we do *see* this circle; the Messianic claim'.[13] The only way in which one can argue with such a vision is by testing its coherence when worked out in detail with all the insights arising from historical, philosophical and religious studies.

But for the moment let me take the concept of 'faith in God through Jesus Christ' as a working definition of what is essential to Christianity and try to push the argument a stage further. And let me begin by spelling out a bit more fully how I understand such 'faith in God through Jesus Christ'. At its heart is the conviction that there is a God of love who is the ultimate source of the world and in whose hands its ultimate destiny lies, that men and women are able to respond to that God and by his grace can be empowered to overcome both the evil of their own sinful devising and that which the world metes out to them. Now that of course is still a very rough and ready statement. To some it will seem minimal, to others it will seem to constitute a very large claim. But I think it expresses the kind of faith in God to which most Christians (whatever else they believe) have been brought through what they have found in Christ, in the scriptures, in the church and in their own experience. Now if that be granted, I then want to ask: Does such a faith in God stand or fall by certain particular historical happenings in the past?

Those who want to insist that it does might seek to establish their point in one of two ways. They may say 'unless the forgiving love of God has actually been embodied in the history of Israel and in the life, death and resurrection of Jesus (the precise form depending on how extensive the history on which they are insisting may be), then your faith in God as a God by whose grace men and women can be empowered to overcome evil must be false; it could not be true'. Or they may make a less dogmatic claim and say: 'Unless it has been embodied in history in that way, then your faith is an insufficiently grounded hypothesis; you would lack reasonable grounds for believing it to be true.'

Let us consider these two lines of argument in turn.

(a) The first, stronger line of argument is not often found explicitly spelt out in recent theological writing. Those who want to affirm most vigorously Christianity's dependence on particular historical events are more inclined to do so on the basis of a positivist view of revelation. For them God has in fact expressed his redemptive love in the life, death and resurrection

of Jesus. That is for them the heart of the matter. Abstract discussion as to whether that redemptive love *could* have found
other expression, less tied to particular historical events, constitutes a form of theological argument that they tend to regard as
improper. Thus Barth is prepared to 'say that God "had to"
become His own Mediator, and therefore "had to" become man,
in order to become manifest to us', but stresses that it would be
an offence against God's freedom to derive such a statement
from general conceptions of God, man and revelation. We
affirm God's revelation in Jesus as necessary only because that is
how he has pleased to reveal himself and even while affirming
its necessity we cannot even deny that it might have pleased
him to reveal himself in some other way as well. I can only say
that such an approach seems to me to beg the question at issue
in a way that I find altogether unconvincing.

(*b*) But the second form of the argument is more common.
The work of John Baker will serve as a representative example of
it. For him God's incarnation in the person of Jesus is essential if
we are to have a reasonable faith in a creative and compassion-
ate God. His position can be most clearly seen in his discussion
of the resurrection. He describes it as 'an objective event', something that can 'reasonably demand our assent . . . as a historical
reality' after 'a detailed historical critique' of the evidence. And
just because it is 'so solid a fact', it can transform the Christian
hope (hope not merely of life after death, but of the ultimate
triumph of the divine purpose for good) from 'hypothesis' to
'faith' or from 'hope' to 'certainty'.[14] You are not justified, he
would object to me (or more accurately he has objected to me in
public discussion) in including the ultimate triumph of the
divine purpose for good in your fundamental faith, unless you
can point to a historical happening such as the resurrection
which is a divine disclosure that this is God's way of working.
Otherwise your faith remains no more than a weakly-grounded
human hypothesis.

Now if the resurrection were a directly given fact – as it was
regarded in the days when the statements of the biblical text and
historical factuality could simply be assumed to coincide –
Canon Baker's argument might have some force. But that is not
our position. The exact historical status of the events traditionally associated with the Christian faith has to be assessed by

historical means and the outcome of that investigation will frequently turn out to be 'non-proven'. We may come down in favour of one possible historical reconstruction, but it will be a balance of possibilities, a choosing of one hypothesis rather than another.

In the situation in which we find ourselves today with regard to the historical witness of the Bible, the difference between the two approaches is much less clear-cut. Admittedly those who believe in the ultimate triumph of the divine purpose for good on the basis of the recorded faith and experience of men and women in the past and of the present experience of themselves and others are making a bold act of faith, for which they can give good grounds but cannot claim certainty. But those who believe in that ultimate triumph of good on the basis of the historical event of Jesus' resurrection are in no better position to claim certainty. The grounding of their faith may seem firmer but the evidence to which they are appealing is only one possible reconstruction from the records. I am not simply repeating Lessing's dictum that the contingent probabilities of historical reconstruction cannot give the certainty that faith requires. Certainty is not available in any case. Even those who insist most strongly on the importance of historicity do not claim that Christian faith can be *proved* thereby. The religious significance (even of the resurrection) is not self-evident, whatever the degree of confidence with which a historical account of it may be established; it has to be seen or grasped with the eye of faith. My claim, therefore, is that there is nothing intrinsically more secure in a knowledge of God which claims to rest on 'certain historical events' whose historicity is regarded as essential than in a knowledge of God which claims to rest on a more general historical experience (including that to which scripture bears witness) but which does not treat any particular events within that broad spectrum as essential.

In conclusion I want to underline what I have tried to argue in this paper, because it is a theme which is very easily liable to misunderstanding and misrepresentation. I have assumed that the scriptural records are not straightforwardly historical accounts, and that in most cases there are a number of possible historical reconstructions between which it is often difficult to choose. But I have not argued for or against either a highly conservative or a highly sceptical view of their historical reliability.

Nor have I argued that the Christian either is or should be uninterested in the question of historicity. Nor again have I argued that the Christian's attitude to his scriptures either is or should be identical in this respect to that of, say, a Hindu to his scriptures. The case that I have been arguing is simply this. Some Christians assert, as a kind of self-evident truth, that Christian faith depends absolutely on the historicity of certain past events; and they see this as something essential to and distinctive of Christianity. I have tried to give reasons for questioning the validity of that particular conviction. That does not commit me to advocating a total divorce between Christianity and history (whatever exactly that would amount to). Of course Christianity derives from certain past events. And the record of those events in scripture (though that is not all that scripture is) continues to be of central importance to the religious life of the Christian church. But the precise way in which it has been understood to be important has changed down the ages with the changing patterns of human culture and knowledge. In the past century such changes have particularly affected man's knowledge of and relation to his own past. This has already influenced Christianity's understanding of itself in many ways. I see the attitude I have advocated in this paper as one aspect of that influence.

The practical implications of the enquiry concern the method and spirit of contemporary theological work. The theologian is often inclined to put the position in this sort of way: 'Such and such is the unchanging Christian faith. It is vulnerable to history in that its very existence depends on such and such historical events. We therefore need to be able to affirm them with such and such a degree of reasoned historical confidence. Let us hope that our historical studies will enable us to go on doing so.' I am not clear by what criteria the initial analysis of what is essential can be made nor am I happy that the historical work is best done in such a context. Ought we not rather to be saying something like this? 'Our faith emerges from and continues to relate itself to such and such a historical heritage. As Christians we should seek to understand that heritage as fully as we can. One of those forms of understanding is assessing what was the nature of the happenings through which Christianity came to birth, in so far as the evidence enables us to form a responsible historical judgment about them. What we discover by such means is part of the raw material in the light of which our faith judgments have to be made.' That is to say, reflecting on what our historical (and other) researches appear to reveal, we have then to say: 'Such and such is the Christian faith as we are in a position to affirm it in our day.' The criteria by which we make such a faith judgment will be no easier to determine than those by which people have sought to assess what is essential to Christian faith. That is a part of the nature of faith. Yet there are advantages in the approach that I am advocating. It makes it more likely that in making our faith judgments we will be making them on the basis of the best evidence available, and where theologians themselves contribute to the historical study they will have a slightly better chance of avoiding a prejudgment of the issues that concern them.

PART III

6

The Holy Spirit in Christian Theology

'The doctrine of the Holy Spirit remains the least explored and developed part of Christian theology.' So wrote Berdyaev.[1] And most theologians would assent not only with an Amen, but also with some more penitential affirmation as well. But just as a direct assault upon acknowledged sins or failings may not always be the most effective method for overcoming them, so also too direct an attempt to develop the doctrine of the Holy Spirit may not be the most fruitful means of progress.

In the Fourth Gospel Jesus declares that he himself is both the way and the truth. In other words, he is to be understood both as one who points away from himself to the Father and also as one who embodies the ultimate reality in his own person. But in the course of the same discourses he declares of the Holy Spirit that he will not speak on his own authority; his function is to be the glorifier of Christ and the revealer of the things that belong to Christ and to the Father. In other words, his role is described in exclusively mediatorial terms and this may well serve to explain the elusiveness of the concept of the Holy Spirit when we try to deal with it in too isolated or direct a fashion.

I would suggest therefore that our lack of progress in elucidation of the doctrine of the Holy Spirit may very largely have arisen from a tendency to ask the wrong questions. If we ask directly about the divine nature and status of the Holy Spirit, we are led on to speak of a Third Person of the Godhead whose essential characteristic is his procession from one (or both) of the other Two Persons of the Godhead. This would seem to me to be a somewhat unilluminating proposition, whose effective significance has remained obscure throughout the long centuries of Christian history. I do not believe that it is along such lines that fruitful progress lies. We would do better to ask the more indirect question – what light is thrown upon our whole understanding of God and of his dealings with mankind by the fact that we know him under the form of Holy Spirit? A question of that nature seems likely to open up far more fruitful lines of inquiry. My purpose here is to sketch out very tentatively the kind of benefit which might be derived from such an approach.

The holiness of God signifies that absolute transcendence, that indefinable otherness by which God is essentially distinguished from man. The holiness of God as apprehended by Isaiah in his vision in the temple is continually reaffirmed by the Christian not only in the adoring cry of the Sanctus in the liturgy but also in the first petition of the basic Christian prayer that God's name be hallowed. The spirit of God signifies God's communion with man, beginning with primitive stories of the spirit of God coming upon the judges of Israel, through the hopes of Ezekiel for a day when God would put his spirit into the hearts of men, on to the experience of Paul in which God's spirit joins with man's spirit in testifying that we are God's children. Thus to know God as Holy Spirit is to know him as both these things at one and the same time; it is to know him as the absolutely other entering into the most intimate conceivable relationship with man. It is a fundamental understanding of the nature of God of this kind that needs to be and that could be illuminated by a fuller and deeper development of the doctrine of the Holy Spirit.

The importance of this kind of approach to the doctrine of the Holy Spirit can be more fully illustrated by considering its significance for a doctrinal understanding of the means of grace, in particular of the word of God and the sacrament of Holy Communion. The inspiration of the Bible is a doctrine most intimately associated with that of the Holy Spirit. Early writers like Justin Martyr can speak simply of Father, Son and prophetic spirit[2] and the fact that he 'spake through the prophets' is enshrined in our basic credal affirmation about the Holy Spirit. There have often been those who have envisaged this inspiration in sub-personal terms after the analogy used by

Athenagoras of the flute-player playing upon a flute.[3] But the truer Christian insight has followed the mind of Origen, who insisted that it was just at this point that Christian inspiration was to be distinguished from pagan. Divine inspiration for him represents not a replacement but a heightening of the powers of the mind.[4] But inspiration does not exhaust the idea of the Holy Spirit's role in our understanding of the Bible as a means of grace. As Origen once more clearly recognized, there is an equal need of the Spirit in the interpretative work of the reader and the exegete. Thus the actual words of the Bible are but one stage in a total process of communion between God and man, which is fundamental to the very nature of God as Holy Spirit. To attempt to isolate the words of the Bible and to define their status in the divine economy is already to remove them from the only context in which they have meaning. It is to be ruled out from the start as something that is incompatible with a true understanding of God as Holy Spirit.

The same principle applies with equal force in our understanding of the sacrament of Holy Communion. Just as the words of the Bible considered in themselves are momentary media in a total work of personal communion with men, so in precisely the same way the elements of bread and wine are to be understood as momentary media in a total work of personal communion between God and man. The difficulties which arise in any attempt to enunciate a theology of the Bible which overlooks this subordinate role of the actual written words similarly threaten much traditional thought about the eucharistic elements. We have seen that it is a misleading approach to separate the words of the Bible as standing midway between the Spirit's two functions of inspiration and interpretation and to try to define their objective status as a distinct entity. So also it is a misleading approach to isolate out the elements of bread and wine as standing midway between consecration and worthy reception and to try to define their distinct objective status. In just the same way the attempt needs to be ruled out from the start as incompatible with a true understanding of God as Holy Spirit.

These illustrations might well appear to show that the approach which I am putting forward would prove destructive altogether of that which is normally spoken of as Christian doctrine. I do not think that this is the case, and I would like to end this article by trying to generalize what its significance might be for the work of doctrinal theology as a whole.

Theology is concerned in the first instance with God himself and secondly with the means of God's dealings with men. In the first case we do normally recognize the lack of precision which necessarily characterizes any attempt to define and to describe. The shortcomings of doctrinal work in this field are most often the abstractness and aridity which seem inevitably to characterize what we have to say, and yet which cannot but seem singularly inapposite and inadequate in an attempt to apprehend the nature of God. In the second case, in those aspects of Christian doctrine which concern the means of grace, we are inclined to believe that we can achieve a far more considerable measure of precision. But precision arises only in so far as we treat the objects of our study as ends in themselves rather than as means of grace, as media of God's dealings with us. Both these difficulties – the aridity of traditional doctrines of God and over-confident precision in other aspects of theological doctrine – arise from a failure to grasp the true character of faith in God as Holy Spirit. If we take this doctrine seriously, then our doctrine of God can never be arid because we shall always have in mind that it is of the very nature of God to be the absolutely other who yet enters most intimately into communion with men. And similarly we shall be saved from over-confident definition in other fields of theology when we recognize that a theological treatment of any of the means of grace – doctrines not only of the Bible and of Holy Communion, but also of church and ministry, of redemption and sanctification – must always see them as integral elements in the total work of the Holy Spirit, that is, of a God who not only humbles himself to behold the things that are in heaven and earth but who even deigns to enter into the closest communion with us.

The traditional approach to the doctrine of the Holy Spirit which I am setting out to criticize here arises, I have argued, from attempting to understand the Holy Spirit in too direct and isolated a manner. This has led to the hypostatization of the idea of the Holy Spirit as a distinct third person of the Godhead. The danger of this approach in relation to our understanding of the nature of God is that it might seem to present that aspect of our understanding of God which comes through our knowledge of him as Holy Spirit as something that is partial, peripheral or secondary in the being of God rather than total, central and primary. This danger has to a very large extent been overcome in the history of Christian doctrine by the insistence upon the absolutely co-equal and undivided nature of the Trinity and by such subtle concepts as the Augustinian doctrine of appropriations. These do provide an effective answer to the difficulty that I have raised but they have their own intrinsic difficulties, which I have tried to deal with elsewhere and which seem to me to be of a very serious nature.[5]

But the traditional approach with its hypostatization of the Holy Spirit has also, in my contention, had a harmful effect upon other aspects of Christian doctrine into which the idea of the Holy Spirit enters, such as the doctrines of the Bible and sacraments. By objectifying the Holy Spirit in our minds, we are led on to try to locate his particular role in the working of the means of grace. His role is therefore seen as inspiration of the scriptural writer or as transforming agent of the sacramental elements at the moment of epiclesis – or in some such analogous way. We are then tempted to go on and describe other parts of those doctrines without reference to the Holy Spirit on the assumption that the Holy Spirit's part in the whole matter has already been described. In this way we only succeed in raising for ourselves problems that at first sight seem capable of clear and explicit answers but which are in fact pseudo-questions incapable of being answered at all in a meaningful way. To hypostatize the Holy Spirit in this way is not to honour him but to tame him; it is to set him upon a pedestal which may seem to be a place of honour, but which is really removing him from effective influence upon the day-to-day stuff of our doctrinal thinking. My claim therefore is that we have totally misunderstood the role of the idea of the Holy Spirit in Christian theology. It is not one more counter to be fitted in on equal terms with the other ideas which are pieced together in the intellectual jig-saw puzzle of our doctrinal thinking. Its role in the game of our intellectual struggle is of a different order. Mention of the Holy Spirit in relation to a particular doctrine should not be understood as the introduction of one more term into the discussion, but rather as a warning note whose significance is to be understood as follows: 'Beware, you are involved in an attempt to understand a part of the whole story of God's dealings with mankind. You are in danger of isolating the little part which is your immediate concern in such a way that you may distort its real significance. The thing that you are trying to understand can only be properly understood in one way – namely in relation to the Holy Spirit, or in other words as a part of the activity of a God who is absolutely transcendent and yet who at the same time enters into the most intimate conceivable fellowship with men.' It is true that such an approach may not always make for very clear-cut, precise and tidy theological formulations, but it would be an invaluable check upon the development of theological systems, which though outwardly impressive, are of little real worth because they offend against the basic principles of true theological method.

7

The Uses Of 'Holy Scripture'

Is 'Holy Scripture' Christian? is certainly a striking title for a theological book.[1] Christopher Evans himself describes it apologetically as a 'perhaps foolish title'.[2] It has a recognizably impish quality about it, but characteristically it poses a question that is searching, even uncomfortable, but far from foolish.

In the course of Christian history the distinctive character of 'holy scripture' has often been asserted in ways which were epistemologically absurd and religiously disastrous. Its composition has been ascribed to forms of dictation which left the human writer no more than an instrument in the hand of the divine author but ensured the inerrancy of the resultant text. Then in obedience to its commands witches have been burnt to the glory of God or else a divine authority claimed for all one's own immediate concerns by the Midas touch of allegorical interpretation. Modern scholarship has learnt long since to eschew all such excesses. But the distinctive character of 'holy scripture' is still frequently linked to accounts of revelation that carry less than universal assent. Christopher Evans gives one such example in his discussion of Cullmann's book *Salvation in History*.[3] Professor Mitchell has recently suggested that if the concept of divine inspiration of the Bible is to be retained, it will need to take the form of a belief 'that there are truths which men could not have discovered by themselves, but which God has found means of communicating to them'.[4] I do not intend to discuss here whether any account of inspiration or revelation of this kind can be sustained which would justify something like the degree of distinctiveness traditionally ascribed to 'holy scripture'. That task is one that appears to me to be a good deal more difficult than it is often assumed to be.

But in this paper I want to pursue a different question. It is this: suppose one were unable to provide any such account, would it follow that one ought to abandon the idea of a canonical scripture altogether? Or would there still be a place for a 'holy book' in the practice of Christian faith? Other religions which have very different ideas of revelation from the Christian tend to have their 'holy books' too. While the particular role of the Christian scriptures is undoubtedly related to the particular Christian understanding of revelation and of the unique incarnation of God in Jesus Christ, it would be surprising if Christianity's holy book did not function within Christianity in ways comparable with the role of holy books in other religious traditions. I propose therefore to offer some rather broad reflections on the way in which a holy book is liable to function in a religious culture, to consider how far the Bible functions in that kind of way and finally to attempt some evaluation of it in relation to those functions. I shall set out my reflections under three headings.

1. *Respect for antiquity*

Change always involves an element of loss. Even where change is clearly desirable, the past was seldom wholly evil and past good is often lost (it may be inevitably) along with the excision of the evil. Enthusiastic supporters of the New English Bible will normally be prepared to admit that where it replaces the Authorized Version there is loss as well as gain. In a preliterate society where change is slow and the greatest danger is loss of old skills, religion is likely to fulfil an important conservative role. The myths speak of a golden age in the past, and much religious practice is designed to preserve or recapture it. Writing is an enormously important tool for this kind of preservative function. Books, when they first began to appear, would have had, in addition to their practical value, an aura of rarity and mystery which they cannot possibly have for us in an age of the paperback and the popular press. I remember a Nigerian student at the University of Ibadan, himself a first generation literate, telling me of the sense of shock with which in his first weeks at the University he had heard one of his tutors say that he did not agree with what a published book said. His sense of shock was very similar to that which a fundamentalist Christian might feel on hearing for the first time someone say that he thought the Bible was wrong in some particular respect.

The charge of novelty is a powerful weapon of attack in making a religion look ridiculous. Celsus used it against Christianity; Roman Catholics (in less ecumenical days) used to use it against Protestants; and main-line Protestants use it against Christian Scientists and Jehovah's Witnesses. The Old Testament scriptures were important to the infant Christian church not only for internal guidance, but as a way of providing external respectability, of showing that Christianity was a religion with a past. On the whole people don't write 'scripture'; they write (very possibly believing themselves to be doing so by inspiration of the Spirit), but time has to pass before what they have written becomes 'scripture'. If they want to write scripture they do so pseudepigraphically in the name of some past saint or hero, or else they find it conveniently hidden in the temple.

Thus a written record hints at the changeless, primeval character of religion; it suggests that religion is concerned with the eternal rather than the ephemeral. It is a standing corrective against the shallowness of a religion that in its passionate concern with the present moment has lost its hold on that dimension.

That is an important function; and a religion without holy scriptures would be in grave danger of losing something vital. But can they fulfil that role without at the same time doing even greater harm? New knowledge arises; moral standards change (often for the better). The immorality of Homer's gods, for example, came to be regarded as intolerable. His poems as a result were to be excluded from Plato's ideal republic and he himself consigned (as in Pythagoras' dream) to Hades, where he was depicted suspended from a tree and surrounded by serpents, together with those who had neglected their wives, because of the things he had said about the gods.[5] Alternatively his lively stories could be allegorized into cosmogonical myths as by the Stoics. Christians too have often become involved in similar spiritual contortions, and indeed still do so to this day as pious congregations find themselves exulting in the hope of vengeance upon Babylon and singing, 'Blessed shall he be that taketh thy children and throweth them against the stones.'[6]

But there are other, less obvious, dangers too. Plato's suspicion of books, that characterized his later years, was more broadly based than simply on his objection to the immorality of Homer's gods. Books could never fully express the doctrine they were intended to convey; some readers were sure to misunderstand them and the book was unable to defend or to explain itself.[7] Moreover once books come to be revered as authorities, they encourage false short-cuts to knowledge. A. D. Nock declared that 'throughout the imperial period one of the conspicuous features of intellectual life is a readiness to accept statements because they were in books or even because they were said to be in books'.[8] So in later centuries the writings of Aristotle were regarded as rendering otiose the careful observations of the naturalist. Once grant that your book has the authority of God himself and such tendencies will be further exaggerated. Economic research and moral enquiry are not of central importance if the holy book already contains for you the essential insights into the proper ordering of society and an unchanging code of ethical behaviour. The use of the Bible to strengthen the forces of reaction is written large on the pages of history.

Now there is of course much else within the pages of the Bible that not only permits but insists on radical change. The New Testament's critique of the Old carries within it an implicit protest against the very way in which it has itself so often been regarded in the past. That respect for the past which the very existence of a holy scripture embodies and makes effective must for the Christian be dialectically combined with the ruthless criticism of life lived in the Spirit, that wind whose source and destination no man can tell.

2. *Escape from subjectivity*

For the most part the religious believer has (or should have) a healthy distrust of his own subjective judgments. He seeks escape from the smallness and the sinfulness implicit in a purely private, personal perspective. His faith is in that which is other than and greater than himself. He longs for objectivity, a sense of his faith as something given rather than something self-induced. So he sees holy scripture not merely as something coming to him with the givenness that belongs to the past as a whole; it is in some special way given by God. Thus the Old

Testament law was not only found in the temple, some of it at least was written with the finger of God. A part of the Egyptian *Book of the Dead* was similarly found under a statue of the god Thoth and written in the writing of the god himself.[9] The Qur'an too was dictated by the angel Gabriel; and, as if that were not sufficient, later tradition (in direct contradiction of the text of the Qur'an itself) went on to recount how Muhammad ascended into heaven and received it directly from the very hands of God.[10]

But however strong the insistence on a direct divine source of holy scripture, it has never long been possible to avoid a balancing emphasis on the need for divine illumination of the reader also. Thus the Calvinist tradition has emphasized the need for the *'testimonium internum spiritus sancti'* and we find a Muslim Sufi declaring that 'no understanding of the Holy Book is possible until it is actually revealed to the believer as it was revealed to the prophet'.[11]

Such developments force us to ask how effectively a written record can fulfil its role as a source of genuine objectivity. Men certainly can evade its force by allegorical or other means and often do so, albeit unconsciously. Nevertheless it is some sort of check. It takes some getting round. Words have a firmer shape of meaning than symbolic acts or visual representation. And this, I take it, is at least a part of what lies behind the insistence of the Reformed tradition on the primacy of audition over against vision as the model by which knowledge of God ought to be construed – a theme much emphasized by Professor Torrance in his recent writings.[12] Words, and still more written words, have a tougher element of objectivity about them. We may be able to escape their implications by self-deception, but we would deceive ourselves more easily without them.

In the *Confessions* of Augustine there is an instructive discussion which serves to show how limited this provision of objectivity is. It is easier, he argues, to be confident of the fact of God's creation of all things visible and invisible than it is to be certain of what Moses intended by the opening verses of the book of Genesis. Our primary concern therefore has to be with what is true rather than with what is the meaning of the written text. He goes on:

> When [a man] says 'Moses did not mean what *you* say, but what *I* say,' and then does not deny what either of us says but allows that *both* are true – then, O my God, life of the poor, in whose breast there is no contradiction, pour thy soothing balm into my heart that I may patiently bear with people who talk like this! It is not because they are godly men and have seen in the heart of thy servant what they say, but rather they are proud men and have not considered Moses' meaning, but only love their own – not because it is true but because it is their own.[13]

We are in no position to tell how fair Augustine is being to his critics. But there is no denying the shrewdness of his psychological insight.Men do undoubtedly read back their own meanings into the sacred text. And their capacity for doing so, albeit in good faith and without, at least at the conscious level, the perverted motives which Augustine ascribes to his opponents, is no harmless eccentricity. For having once convinced themselves that their meaning is the objective meaning of the sacred text, they then hold it with a renewed fanaticism as something which comes to them with the direct authority of God himself. It is a high price to pay for something that originates in a proper desire to escape from the dangers of subjectivity.

The question that then forces itself upon us is this. Can we be free of such dangers while still holding on to 'holy scripture' as a *symbol* of that objectivity, that otherness, that address to us which is at the heart of faith in a personal God? If we should no longer find it possible to see the Bible as characterized by that distinctive form of divine address which theories of inspiration have attempted to delineate, or if we have already become fully aware of the way in which any such divine address is inextricably intermingled with the fallibility of its human form both in its original expression and in its interpretation, can the concept of 'holy scripture' still fulfil such a role even symbolically? Or would any such idea be more likely to mislead than to serve the cause of truth?

3. *Focus on community*

Homer may have been consigned by Pythagoras to Hades, but the primary school-children of the Hellenistic world were made to inscribe in their exercise books, as their first essay in writing, the words 'Homer was not a man but a god'.[14] The poetic tradition, with Homer at its heart, provided for the Hellenistic age 'a fundamental homogeneity which made communication and genuine communion easier'. Men had in common 'the same metaphors, images, words – the same language'.[15] It ensured a basic unity of culture, in much the same way that the Bible and Shakespeare did in England a hundred years ago.[16]

In the same sort of way a fixed canon (like a fixed liturgy) provides a focus of unity for the Christian community, a common source of religious imagery; it needs to be large enough to provide for the rich variety of men's religious needs but compact enough to function as a source of common sensibility.

Its importance as a unifying agent can be illustrated historically. The fixing of the Mosaic canon is linked with Ezra's rebuilding of the Jewish state in conscious opposition to the surrounding peoples. It is no coincidence that the final fixing of the Jewish canon follows so swiftly on the heels of the fall of Jerusalem. The creation of the Christian canon was connected with the need to deal with the threats posed by Marcionites and by Gnostics.

But that method of securing unity over against the challenge of heretical ideas has its limitations. It is a card you can play only once. Having made the canon large enough to rule out Marcion and selective enough to deal with the Gnostics, there was need to find some other way of responding to the later challenges of an Arius or a Luther.

But there are more subtle dangers than those associated with the problem of heresy. The literary canon that is compact enough to be the basis of a common culture is unlikely to be rich enough to sustain that role indefinitely. The kind of situation which may then arise is vividly depicted by Peter Brown in his description of the Roman writer in the age of Augustine:

> Such a man lived among fellow-connoisseurs who had been steeped too long in too few books. He no longer needed to be explicit; only hidden meanings, rare and difficult words and elaborate circumlocutions, could save his readers from boredom, from *fastidium*, from that loss of interest in the obvious, that afflicts the overcultured man ... Above all, the narrow canon of acknowledged classics had been charged with a halo of 'Wisdom': an intellectual agility quite alien to modern man, would have to be deployed constantly to extract the

inexhaustible treasure that, it was felt, must lie hidden in so cramped a quarry.[17]

The natural outcome for the Christian writer in Augustine's day was the regular use of fanciful interpretations of an allegorical kind. But in eschewing the vagaries of allegorical method, we have not thereby freed ourselves from the fundamental problem. Are not some of the difficulties faced by the Roman writer whom Peter Brown describes shared by the authors of the continuous stream of biblical commentaries today? Do not many New Testament interpreters find themselves more or less forced into putting forward far-fetched interpretations in the desperate hope of saying something new, of being 'original' in the sense demanded by examinations for the Doctorate of Philosophy? The way in which a fixed canon provides a shared resource of faith and spirituality for all Christians is a blessing, but it is a mixed blessing.

These are not, of course, the only functions that holy scripture might serve in Christian faith. I have not attempted to explore uses of scripture which arise primarily from the distinctiveness of Christianity. But they seem to me to be three significant ways in which holy books in general, and the Bible in particular, have functioned. All three are religiously important functions which ought to find a place within the life of the church, even though they also have their inherent dangers. If 'holy scripture' is given too absolute a position, then the good that it can convey is likely to be outweighed by the evil that it can also bring with it. But it does not need to be given an absolutist position for the fulfilment of these three roles.

If then these are proper ways of understanding the role of holy scripture within Christian faith, what implications do they have for the interpretation of scripture? The Bible, we are sometimes told, should be studied and interpreted as any other book. That demand is one way of expressing the insistence that the Bible must not be exempted in deference to false piety from all appropriate forms of critical enquiry. But it is not a very satisfactory way of making the point. For how does one interpret 'any other book'? We do not interpret all books identically. To interpret a legal statute is not the same thing as to interpret a novel. They exist for different purposes and we therefore ask different questions of them in the two processes, although we use the one word 'interpretation' for them both.

What then would be involved in interpreting the Bible as 'holy scripture' in the light of the reflections that I have been pursuing here? It would mean discussing it and drawing out its meaning in ways which would enable it to function for us in the three ways that I have tried to describe. This would involve first of all letting it recall for us the primeval nature of those religious traditions out of which our faith comes and for which God cares as fully as he cares for us and for the future. There would be no call to feel ashamed of or try to cover up elements that seem to us strange or crude because they belong to the comparatively primitive origins of religious belief. These would not be in conflict with its role as holy scripture; they would be a proper part of it.

Secondly it would involve letting the Bible symbolize for us the 'over-against-ness' of God. This role stands closest to the traditional understanding of its authority as conveying otherwise inaccessible and wholly reliable knowledge of God. How can such a role continue in a symbolic way once we have come to recognize the need to use our critical judgment and discrimination in determining what is true and what is applicable to our own situation in the biblical record? We would need to be able to see it as something which addresses us in ways that we could not have thought up or invented for ourselves. That is a characteristic of all great literature and of any worthwhile account of occasions of great significance from past history – and clearly on any account the Bible is both those things. It would involve in addition the conviction that the literature and the events recorded are of a kind which (whatever else they may have done) have given rise to true belief about and response to God and have the potentiality of continuing to do so.

Thirdly it would involve seeing the Bible as a common resource of life and spirituality, the provider of a unity of feeling among Christian people. To facilitate its use in this way, what would be called for would be an imaginative development and assimilation of its leading themes and images. This is something that could co-exist (as indeed to some extent it already does) with very great diversity of specific beliefs. No canon, as we have seen, can ever fulfil such a function perfectly. Any selec-

tion of writings as an agreed corpus for such a purpose is bound
to be somewhat arbitrary. But nor is it something than can be
artificially determined by decree from on high. Attempts of that
kind to impose a canon are doomed to failure. It is something
that has to grow. In the canon of scripture the Christian church
has such a growth. Seen in this context the restriction of the
canon might more readily be grasped as blessing and not the
'curse of the canon' that Christopher Evans himself has been
heard on occasion to describe it.

Critical study of the Bible has often been felt to be in conflict
with its role as 'holy scripture'. So, on certain understandings of
what constitutes something 'holy scripture', it has often been. It
does not cohere readily with the conception that a holy book is
first and foremost an authoritative utterance of special divine
origin. But in relation to the uses that I have outlined here it
would more readily appear as a tool in the service of 'holy scripture'.

8

Eucharistic Theology – The Value of Diversity

The so-called sacrament of unity has been a notorious cause of Christian division. Is the eucharist a sacrifice? In what sense is Christ specially present in it? Issues of this kind have divided Christians bitterly from one another. Other contributions to *Thinking about the Eucharist* consider how such issues may be approached today in a more eirenical spirit. The aim of this paper is to ask whether a wide diversity in eucharistic understanding and practice is not only an acceptable aim but also a highly appropriate one. Just as there is widespread agreement today that no one approach to theology can claim absolute priority over all others, so we ought to expect and even to welcome the same sort of variety in eucharistic thought and piety.

Such an enquiry does well to begin at the beginning: Why do we have sacraments at all? In particular, why this one? The appropriateness of a ritual action of this kind at the heart of religious practice appears less obvious to many people today than has often been the case in the past. Yet it is not difficult to point to a wide-spread urge amongst human beings to join together in patterned corporate activity. Such forms of activity are not characteristic only of a primitive stage of social development. In very differing ways they are a feature of all societies at every stage of development. Sacramental activity as a whole has a grounding in the nature of man as created by God.

The basic constituents of such corporate activity are various – processions, dancing, sharing a common meal and so on. What is the significance of the church's concentration upon one particular form of sacramental activity as central to her corporate life? Here the historical link with Jesus and the early church is decisive. Even for those who are led by critical examination of the evidence to question the propriety of speaking of the eucharist as specifically instituted by Jesus, this historical link remains a clear and central factor. But even if this is what is decisive, might not the eucharist still be able to draw more widely than it does upon the varied forms of corporate activity which are natural to human societies? If, for example, the eucharist is intended to provide an expression and experience of joy and fellowship, it might seem that in our contemporary culture dancing and relaxed conversation over a drink are the most natural ways in which to make that provision. Within the liturgy there are admittedly words and actions intended to fulfil this role, but their conventional form often prevents the effective communication of these realities to us. The evaluation of a contemporary eucharistic rite ought not to be made in terms of how far it incorporates strands to be found in earlier rites but rather how far it gives expression to the underlying intentions and objectives of the eucharist. The church could not of course simply replace the eucharist with dancing and relaxed conversation, however effective they might prove in fostering joy and fellowship; for the joy and fellowship which the church seeks to promote is not just any joy and fellowship but one which derives from a response to God as made known in Jesus. The central act with the bread and wine in association with Jesus is irreplaceable if the sacramental activity is to retain its distinctively Christian meaning, but there may well be scope for its linking with a broader complex of other forms of sacramental action.

It is with this distinctive meaning of the eucharist that we must begin. In very general terms it is to be seen as expressing the given nature of the gospel; it shows that the heart of faith is a response and a receiving. This basic insight can be developed in two related but distinguishable ways.

Most obvious is its givenness as a historical phenomenon. Sacramental meals in general may have a basis in common human needs; the eucharistic sacrament derives from one particular form of such meals within the life of Judaism. Moreover, it imposes upon the particular form of sacramental meal a very specific reference to Jesus and to his death and resurrection. It is for this reason that the church has always insisted on the complementary nature of word and sacrament. In terms of practice this has been interpreted with differing degrees of rigour. It has been taken to imply that there should always be a sermon at every celebration of the eucharist; that there should always be a reading from scripture or from the gospel; that the words of institution should always be spoken. In whatever form it is implemented, the essential point is the same. The symbolism of bread and wine is capable of a wide variety of interpretation. A signification in terms of the death of Jesus is not clearly implicit in the symbols themselves. Unless accompanied (at least as a matter of normal practice) by some spoken expression of that signification, it could very easily take on quite other, even contradictory, significance. Thus it seems to be word and sacrament together that are needed to express the historical givenness of the gospel. But it still remains a very open question: how much is given with this historical character of the sacrament? The present hermeneutical debate about how to interpret the words of the gospel today is directly relevant here. It is widely agreed that the words of the gospel do not convey a clear, unchanging meaning which can be directly apprehended by us today; they have to be reinterpreted in the light of our present knowledge about the world and contemporary ways of experiencing it. So the word which accompanies the sacramental action and helps to give it its specifically Christian meaning does not give it an absolutely clear and precise meaning. It, too, requires continual reinterpretation in the same way as does the gospel text as a whole. Thus the extent of what is given in the historical character of the sacrament must not be overstated, though it certainly points to a gift of God mediated to us through the person of Jesus.

But the eucharist may also be seen as pointing in a more general way to the priority of divine grace in the experience of faith. It is possible – and indeed perfectly proper – to speak of our attempt to lay hold of that reality beyond ourselves which we call God. But faith has never been content with this perspective. Part perhaps of the intention of strong forms of a doctrine of the real presence of Christ in the sacrament has been the desire to stress that God is there, making himself present to us prior to all our attempts to lay hold of him. For many people today such a belief does not come easily – especially not in any of its more traditional forms. When the present time is spoken of as a 'non-religious' age, the intention of such language is to stress how difficult it is for very many today to acknowledge the presence or activity of a transcendent God. Moreover, in the light of an increasingly sympathetic understanding of other religions, we tend to be particularly suspicious of accounts of that presence or activity of God which limit him too narrowly to the realm of Christendom, and within specifically Christian thought suspicious of accounts which are too closely tied to particular moments within the experience of the Christian community. Yet in spite of all our difficulty in acknowledging a transcendent personal reality beyond ourselves, in spite of all our dissatisfaction with past ways of expressing God's special activity towards us, we still wish to give expression to our sense of responding to God's initiative, of finding him present before we seek him. And here the symbolism of the eucharist is of great value. At its climax something is given to us. Our role is to receive. The symbolism does not necessarily imply an inroad from beyond ourselves within the rite. It can be understood without the transcendent dimension; it can be seen and experienced simply in terms of a mutual sharing at the human level. But it does lend itself to effective expression of God's prior self-giving to us. At a time when many people find such ideas religiously central but intellectually difficult to express, their embodiment in ritual action is something of especial importance.

Here, then, are two ways in which the symbolism of the eucharist can be seen to point to the givenness of the gospel. But I say 'can be seen'. The symbolism does not express such notions unambiguously or unmistakably. Symbolism never functions in that precise kind of way. The significance has to be apprehended within the symbolic action and drawn out from it. This means that there is no escape from the task of interpretation. Whenever we perform the rite, we have to do it in one particular way; this means that there are also other ways in which we do not do it. Every performance of the rite is an interpretation, whether we are consciously aware of it as such or not. And at this point we may well become aware of differing interpretations, both of which we want to affirm, but which are to some extent in conflict with one another. It may prove impossible in practice to do justice to both at the same time, however much we wish to do so. Two examples may serve to illustrate the point.

Christians affirm both the transcendence and immanence of God, his majesty and his nearness to us. We believe in a God who is wholly other than ourselves, beyond all conceiving, whose very existing is of a different mode or order from our own, but a God who is also closer to us than breathing itself, who has come to us in the person of Christ, who is known to us as and in our neighbour. Critics of Christianity have often objected that such conflicting conceptions introduce a logical incoherence into the Christian idea of God. While not succumbing to those objections we ought not to underestimate their force. It is certainly open to question whether we can give full expression to both poles of that belief in a single pattern of thought or in a single act of worship. A solemn mass at the high altar of a great cathedral may give expression to one; the small group gathered around the table in a house church to the other. The matter is not, of course, as simple as that contrast might suggest. It is possible for the two to be grasped together in some degree – not just as a compromise but as an experience transcending any intellectual synthesis of the two. An awareness of what has been called 'the transcendent in our midst' is not an impossibility. But the point remains that any way of celebrating the eucharist is bound to put its weight more one way than the other. This is at least one element in the difference of feeling that many people have experienced, between the 1662 service and Series 2 – and those two rites are hardly at opposite ends of the scale when one considers the full range of differing forms of eucharistic liturgy.

A second example presents the problem in a more direct and striking form. The material elements of bread and wine give forceful expression to historical continuity; they portray an identification with the action of Jesus at the Last Supper. This aspect has been so strongly felt at times by some that people have insisted not only on bread and wine, but on *unleavened* bread and *fermented* wine. But from a very early stage the elements have also been interpreted as expressive of the incarnational principle; they have been interpreted as an offering of the first fruits of man's labour, as revealing the way in which God uses and transforms the most ordinary and everyday things of our life. But they cannot symbolize this second concept in a time or place where bread or wine is not a staple commodity of the people. So the question is raised from time to time whether it might not be more appropriate in certain circumstances to use within the eucharist sandwiches and beer or rice and saké. In practice the church has remained absolutely firm on this issue. This is no doubt due primarily to the great importance which it attaches to the historical link. It may also derive from the fact that any change at this point would tend to destroy the historical symbolism almost entirely, whereas the incarnational symbolism can always be sustained in some measure – even if not in full measure – with the use of bread and wine. Nevertheless, it is clear that we have here another case of competing symbolisms. In making our choice for one aspect, we may find ourselves reluctantly but inescapably weakening some other.

The approach to the eucharist being suggested here may be illustrated by an analogy with the multiplicity of meanings to be found in Beethoven's string quartets. Their central importance for music is generally agreed. Yet it is hard to formulate what they mean in words, precisely because they are already formulated in music. So the eucharist should be expected to have a wide range of interpretation. This does not mean that there cannot be false interpretations. The wide range of admissible interpretations of the string quartets does not mean that there are not ways of taking them which are quite wrong. So there may be ways of interpreting the eucharist which must be excluded as wrong – ways, for example, which omit the transcendent dimension or the redemptive element altogether. But it does mean that no one interpretation can be claimed as the true interpretation, thereby excluding all others which cannot be fully harmonized with it.

This conviction may serve to throw light on the puzzling question whether some particular occasion is or is not a eucharist. It suggests that the form of the question is a misleading one if it is being asked with the intention of drawing a hard and fast line between what is and what is not a eucharist. It may still be of value if its intention is to help us clarify what are important features of eucharistic worship which we should expect to find there as a norm – but none of which need necessarily be required as essential for ensuring that it is a eucharist with which we have to do. Two examples from contemporary discussion may illustrate the point.

Can there be eucharists without an ordained minister as celebrant? The issue arises not only between episcopal and non-episcopal churches. Might there not be occasions when a group of Christians, not happening to include an ordained minister among their number, were engaged upon some common enterprise in the course of which it seemed highly appropriate for them (with no schismatic intention) to break bread together? Rather than consider whether such an occasion was or was not a eucharist, it might be better to indicate the ways in which if fulfilled some important aspects of eucharistic symbolism but not others. The presidency of an ordained minister at the eucharist is important because it gives expression (like the unchanging character of the elements) to the historical givenness of the sacrament; moreover, by virtue of his authorized and representative status the ordained minister is a reminder of the relationship of any particular grouping of Christians to the whole body of the church. But it is not self-evidently the case that an occasion which lacks this particular element in the total complex of eucharistic symbolism but contains perhaps many other features is *ipso facto* not a eucharist. It may deviate from the norm without necessarily ceasing thereby to be a eucharist.

A slightly different form of the same problem arises in the ecumenical context in the common worship of Christians of different confessions. Questions have been asked about the sort of distinction which we ought to make between occasions when a breaking of bread is a eucharist and occasions when it is an *agape*. The most obvious difference between the two is that between the ritual eating and drinking characteristic of the former and the sharing of the full meal in the case of the latter. It is customary to lay great stress on the importance of maintaining a very firm distinction of kind between them. But both can trace their ancestry to early eucharistic practice and both can be shown to have positive, though differing, sacramental value. May there not be a case for laying an equal stress on the possibility of both having a valuable place within the totality of a varied eucharistic practice?

What is being suggested here is in line with what has already to some degree happened in relation to the docrine of the church. It used to seem self-evident (perhaps indeed to some it still does) that in the face of ecclesiastical division the appropriate question to ask is: Which body (or bodies) is (or are) the church and which are not? The Roman Catholic church allowed the claim only for herself; Anglicans tended to a theory which included the Roman Catholic, Orthodox and Anglican Communions, but no other – and so on. But in course of time so much was granted in terms of God's grace operating in other Christian bodies outside the true church, that the distinction between what was and what was not the church became little more than an arbitrary semantic decision. Sometimes an attempt has been made to maintain the distinction in a somewhat less rigid way by differentiating between the church and other ecclesial bodies. So in this case also the sharpness of the distinction might be softened by speaking of the eucharist over against other eucharistic activities. But that kind of distinction does not seem to offer a satisfactory resting place. It seems rather to be a kind of transitional stage on the way to a wholly different way of understanding the problem of division. Thus in relation to the church there are many today who would prefer to speak in terms of the degree to which differing Christian bodies do or do not express in their life and structure the marks to be looked for in the church as a norm. Those marks, combining as they do such contrasting elements as order and freedom, catholicity and indigenous expression, are not easily to be found harmoniously expressed in any single body. In a similar way we need perhaps to become less concerned with drawing boundaries of what is or is not a genuine eucharist and more ready to ask in what varied ways we can today give expression to that rich range of religious reality which is offered to us in the whole eucharistic tradition.

No attempt in this short paper has been made to undertake that task. Its purpose is simply to suggest a more flexible way of approaching eucharistic theology, which might help us to grasp the meaning of the eucharist not only in a more eirenical way, but at the same time with greater fullness and depth.

9

Sacramental Unity in the Early Church

The problem of intercommunion is a contemporary problem which cannot be solved by parallels and precedents from the days of the early church, for there are none. But the particular problem of intercommunion is part of a wider issue – the relation of communion worship to the unity of the church. This was not the most prominent issue in the early church's thought about the eucharist, but it was an important part of it. Standard works on the development of eucharistic doctrine tend to stress the ways in which the understanding of it as heavenly food and as the Christian sacrifice took shape in the life and conscious-ness of the church. It seems therefore that there may be some value in a study which seeks to isolate, so far as that can legiti-mately be done, early thought about the eucharist in relation to the unity of the church.

The unity of the church in the thought of the New Testament is something both local and universal. The two were not neces-sarily or theoretically in conflict, though tension could easily arise between them as the relationship between the Jerusalem and Gentile churches bears witness. Action which made for unity within a local Gentile church might be a source of rupture between that church as a whole and the churches of Judaea. Both kinds of unity mattered to St Paul. Divisions within the church of Corinth or within the church as a whole were equally abhorrent to him. I do not think that one ought to say that one is more important than the other for him. But it is worth noticing that what I have described as a division within the church as a whole would more naturally be described by Paul as division between the churches.[1] There was certainly for him a single people of God but when speaking of 'the church' his direct reference is normally to the single congregation. Too much should not be made of this which is primarily a linguistic point, but it ought not to be overlooked altogether in an age when it is sometimes implied that it is a little improper to use the word 'church' except of the church universal.

But however they be described both kinds of division were dangers known to Paul and both were to him false divisions of essential unities. Furthermore in both cases Paul sought to overcome the difficulty not merely by exhortation and reminder of the existing unity but by sacramental expression of it. The importance which he attached to the collection for the poor saints at Jerusalem (an issue which was sometimes a source of strain and embarrassment to him in his relationship with the churches of his own foundation) was the fact that it gave tangible expression to the mutual interdependence of the church. The Jerusalem church might have its doubts about the full validity of the uncircumcised Gentile churches, but that was no justification for the Gentile churches to go it on their own. Rather it enhanced the importance of their provision for the practical needs of the Jerusalem church, not as a form of spiritual blackmail but as a voluntarily chosen and clearly visible expression of the church's real unity in Christ.[2] Mutual Responsibility and Interdependence within the Anglican communion was intended to be not a matter of mere financial convenience but also a sacrament of unity.

No mention is made in this wider context of the eucharist as a sacrament of unity. It is with regard to divisions within the local community that the eucharist is affirmed to fulfil this role. Indeed it is only at that level that it can properly be said to fulfil the role sacramentally at all. It is only the members of the local congregations who can be said in the literal meaning of the words 'to partake of the one loaf'. The fact that other congregations in other parts of the world practise the same sacramental rite may be an important expression of unity, but it is only in a secondary sense a sacramental expression of unity. The expression is only sacramental in a primary sense for those who actually 'partake of the one loaf'. It is in this context and in this sense that Paul emphasizes so strongly the unitive significance of sacramental participation in the one loaf of communion worship.

What is true here of Paul is true, I believe, also of the patristic age in general. This is not to claim that the unity of the church universal was denied or regarded as of little importance; that I believe would be false. But it is to claim that the role of the eucharist as a sacramental expression of unity belonged far more to the context of local church unity than to that of the unity of the worldwide church.

Essentially the same picture with the same balance between emphasis on the local and the universal emerges from the writings of Ignatius as from the writings of Paul. Ignatius is well known as the first writer to speak explicitly of the 'catholic' or 'universal' church. The concept is a real and important one for him, but it is not the direct or central concern in his writing. His primary insistence is on the need for the unity of the local church as a bulwark against the vagaries of heresy.

This local unity finds its focal expression in the person of the bishop. This is more than a mere matter of expediency. The single figure of the bishop is for Ignatius a kind of sacramental expression of the unity of God. The true Christian penitent returns 'to the unity of God and the council of the bishop' (*Philadelphians* 8), and it is clear enough that in Ignatius's view it would be impossible to do the former without the latter. The bishop is therefore a focus of unity for church life in all its aspects. 'Let no man do aught of the things pertaining to the church apart from the bishop' (*Smyrnaeans* 8).

But within 'the things pertaining to the church' which are to be held together by their unfailing relation to the person of the bishop, the eucharist clearly holds a very special place. The sentence just quoted from the letter to the Smyrnaeans is followed by the words: 'Let that be held a valid eucharist which is under the bishop or one to whom he shall have committed it.' The condemnation of any eucharist not under the bishop or his delegate does not appear to be related to any special authority which has been transmitted to the bishop in succession but solely to him as the sacramental expression of the unity of God and therefore of the church.

The point is made more emphatically with relation to the eucharist in *Philadelphians* 4: 'Be careful therefore to observe one eucharist (for there is one flesh of our Lord Jesus Christ and one cup into union in his blood; there is one altar, as there is one bishop, together with the presbytery and the deacons my fellow-servants) that whatsoever you do, you may do it after God.' The oneness of the eucharist follows both from the oneness of the Christ whose flesh it is and from the oneness of the bishop (himself expressing the oneness of God) apart from whom it may not validly be celebrated.

Now one of the characteristics of the heretics, whom Ignatius sees as a threat to the church, was their abstention from the eucharist. It does not seem that they were abstaining for primarily schismatic reasons in order to have their own eucharist apart from the bishop, but rather that for docetic reasons they were unwilling to practise a sacramental eucharist at all. 'They abstain from eucharist and prayer, because they allow not that the eucharist is the flesh of our Saviour Jesus Christ, which flesh suffered for our sins, and which the Father of his goodness raised up' (*Smyrnaeans* 6). These men are clearly church members (otherwise one could not speak of their 'abstaining' from the eucharist) who deliberately do not attend the church's eucharist for reasons of doctrinal conviction of a spiritualistic or docetic kind. With this rejection of the material aspect of Christian worship went also, according to Ignatius, a failure in the material aspect of Christian love in practical care for the widow, the orphan and the afflicted. In Ignatius's view this kind of failure is utterly incompatible with any semblance of true Christianity, however much the heretics may continue to name the name of Christ. Those who cut themselves off from association with the church's eucharist are to be cut off by the members of the church from any kind of association whatever. 'It is therefore meet that you should abstain from such, and not speak of them either privately or in public' (*Smyrnaeans* 7).

Thus the bishop is the essential focus of the unity of the local church. That local unity also finds expression of an almost equally important kind in the eucharist. Yet the unity of the one eucharist is in some measure derivative from the unity of the bishop apart from whom it cannot validly exist. But there does not appear to be for Ignatius any comparable focus or sacramental expression of the wider unity of the universal church. It is widely accepted that the fact that Ignatius does not mention any bishop in his address to the church of Rome is evidence that there was no single bishop of that church at that time. Yet there is certainly no suggestion that Ignatius regards it for that reason as any less a true part of the church universal. The wider unity of the church could exist validly 'apart from the bishop', without, that is to say, there needing to be a bishop in every place to give expression to it. Ignatius does not seem to look for any other expression of the wider church unity than the person of Christ himself. His oft-quoted reference to the 'catholic' church comes in that very section of the letter to the Smyrnaeans (8) where he asserts the invalidity of any eucharist – or other church activity – done apart from the bishop. He writes: 'Wheresoever the bishop shall appear, there let the people be; even as where Jesus may be, there is the universal church.' The sacramental expression of unity is for him a matter of the local church. This is clearly true of its primary representation in the person of the bishop. It seems also to be true of the secondary, but still very important, representation of it in the one eucharist. This, too, as the sacramental character of the one loaf would lead us to expect, is essentially expressive of the unity of the congregation assembled to share it together.

So far I have been drawing a firm line of distinction between the unity of the local church and the unity of the church universal. But the two concepts cannot be kept at arm's length from one another. In two ways in particular the interrelation of the two came to the fore in the course of the second century. In the first place the local church cannot be easily and without question identified with the single congregation gathered around the one loaf. In a small provincial town with comparatively few Christians the identification is obvious enough. But in the larger cities with growing numbers it is not so straightforward. Numbers might become too large for the regular gathering of all Christians together in one place, while the city might still be the only obvious unity in terms of which it would be natural to conceive the local church. So there would arise a local church with more than one eucharistic gathering. In the second place Christians of a particular tradition and nationality who had moved to some other place would feel a sense of belongingness to the church of their origin and upbringing as well as to the church of their new home. Both these problems were particularly acute in Rome, the largest city of the empire, and also one with a highly cosmopolitan population drawn from all quarters of the known world. It is within the context of these problems that the so-called 'quartodeciman controversy' of the second century is to be understood.

The substance of the controversy can be told quite briefly. There were living in Rome in the second century a substantial number of Christians of Asiatic origin. The tradition of the church in Asia was to observe the Christian paschal celebration on the day of the Jewish Passover, Nisan 14, whereas the Roman Church observed it on the Sunday following. There is no evidence that this divergence of custom was felt to be an embarrassment in the middle of the second century as long as the two divergent customs were practised in Asia and Rome respectively. But when the Asiatic Christians insisted on following their local custom in Rome, this was felt in Rome to be a threat to the proper unity of the church there. Nevertheless it was agreed between Anicetus of Rome and Polycarp of Smyrna that the difference of custom should continue, and the two practices existed for a time side by side within the church at Rome. But towards the end of the century Pope Victor made a further and more determined attempt to secure conformity within the church under his authority. We have not the evidence to assess Victor's motives with any confidence. It is possible that he was motivated by an autocratic love of power or by an administrative desire for tidiness. But it is by no means certain that his motives were purely of this order. It may well be that he had a real problem on his hands. Both Marcion and Valentinus had developed their heretical ideas and practices with separatist groups in Rome. An Asiatic group refusing to conform on an issue which, whether justly or not, could well appear suspect on grounds of Judaizing, might well seem – indeed might easily have been – a danger to the well-being of the Roman church. Certainly from whatever motives Victor treated the matter as one of urgency. When the churches of Asia, through their spokesman Polycrates, continued to support the right of the Asiatics in Rome to continue there their own apostolic tradition, Victor tried to have the Asiatic churches as a whole treated as excommunicate by all the other churches of the known world. Victor's threats did not receive full support from the other churches to whom he appealed, even where they may themselves have followed and approved the same pattern of Paschal observance as the church of Rome. The exact course of the dispute is not recorded, but certainly in the long run the Asiatic churches did come to accept the Roman practice.[3]

If this interpretation of the controversy be correct, we have a case in which the need to deal with unity at a local level led on inevitably to consideration of unity at a universal level. Conformity of practice was first insisted on at the local level, but it could not effectively be secured there without a similar conformity of practice in the world-wide church as a whole. The immediate irritant, which gave rise to the wider problem, was the existence of an Asiatic group within the church at Rome holding its own eucharists and in particular holding its most solemn eucharist of the year on a different occasion from other congregations.

This Asiatic group may possible have been the first distinct group with its own eucharistic life in Rome, but the facts of the case at least suggest the possibility that there were a number of other similarly separate congregations. The likelihood of this is strongly supported by certain words of Irenaeus. Irenaeus objected to Victor's attempted coercion of the Asiatics and in the course of a letter to Victor in which he recalls the earlier practice of tolerance in the days of Anicetus and Polycarp, he writes: 'None were ever cast out because of this course of action (i.e. differing date of paschal observance) but those very elders before thee, though they did not observe it, would send the eucharist to members of those communities who observed it.'[4]

The implication of these words of Irenaeus are of particular importance for our present concern. We have seen how the one loaf was expressive of the unity of the congregation which shared it. But the situation soon arose where in a city like Rome the members of the church could not all share in the single eucharistic gathering. Was it possible to give sacramental expression to the unity of the local Christian community where there had to be a number of separate eucharistic celebrations? We know from Justin Martyr that it was customary to express the unity of Christians unable to be present at the eucharistic gathering because of sickness or some similar cause with the church community by sending to them a portion of the consecrated loaf (1 Apology 67). The words of Irenaeus (though not unequivocally explicit) suggest that it was customary to do the same in order to express sacramentally the unity of the separated congregations. We have clear evidence of a practice of this kind in the fourth century. Both Miltiades (311–14) and Siricius (384–99) are recorded as having sent a portion of the consecrated bread, called the 'fermentum', to other churches in the city where the eucharist was being celebrated by presbyters under their jurisdiction.[5] The main emphasis in those records is laid on the act as symbolizing the authority of the Pope over his presbyters. Their authority to celebrate the eucharist was not something which existed independently of their relationship to their bishop. But the original emphasis may well have been more upon the unity of the congregations as Irenaeus words would suggest. Indeed there is really little difference between the two emphases. The complex of ideas – one church, one bishop, one eucharist – belongs closely together as we have seen already in the writings of Ignatius.

Thus the 'fermentum' provided a sacramental means of expression of the unity of the local church, even in the extended sense of that term by which it must be understood to include a number of distinct congregations. How widespread the practice was we have no means of telling. But references to what appears to be a virtually identical custom are to be found in some of the canons of the Eastern Church, showing that it was more than a purely Roman custom. The thirty-second Canon of the Council of Laodicea (mid fourth century: date uncertain), for example, forbids the reception of 'eulogiae' from heretical groups on the ground that they are 'alogiae' (follies) rather than 'eulogiae'.[6] The exact status of the 'eulogiae' here mentioned is a matter of dispute. They may have been a form of blessed bread sent as a gift and not the sacrament itself.[7] But it seems more likely that the bread sent was originally the eucharistic element itself and that the 'eulogiae' of which this canon speaks could still have been in that form. Certainly the practice was a serious expression of communion, which could not rightly be enjoyed with congregations opposed to the church's faith.

Thus there was a way in which the eucharist could provide a sacramental expression of unity beyond the single congregation. It was certainly practised in Rome between the second and fourth centuries, and probably more widely. But there were obvious practical limitations which restricted the extent to which this further expression of sacramental unity could be carried. In particular growing reverence for the consecrated elements themselves made the sending of them on journeys of some distance seem a risky and undesirable custom, and clearly restricted the range of this particular method of expressing a wider sacramental unity. We have evidence of this restriction both from Rome and from the East.

Innocent I (401–17) describes the practice at Rome in his day in a letter to Decentius of Eugubium who had consulted him on a number of practical questions. One of those questions concerned 'the fermentum, which we send to all city churches (per titulos) on the Lord's day'. On this subject Innocent says that 'the presbyters of churches situated inside the city, who are unable to join with us on that day because of the people committed to their care, receive at the hand of acolytes a fermentum which has been prepared by us, so that they may not reckon themselves cut off from communion with us on that day of all days. But I don't think this ought to be done for outlying parishes (per parochias), as the sacrament ought not to be carried too far; nor therefore do we send it to the presbyters who are situated in the more scattered cemeteries, and the presbyters there have the right and permission of doing the rite themselves'.[8] In similar vein the fourteenth Canon of Laodicea decrees that 'the sacred elements (τὰ ἅγια) are not to be sent as a "eulogia" to other παροικίας at the Easter festival'.[9] Exactly what is envisaged by these two passages – especially the very condensed fourteenth Canon of Laodicea – is open to debate. Is it right to translate τὰ ἅγια as 'the sacred elements' or could the phrase refer to some other blessed bread of less than full sacramental character? Does the forbidding of the practice at Easter imply that it was permissible at other times? Or was it, more probably, only practised at Easter and therefore in fact being forbidden altogether? Does παροικία here mean a diocese[10] and therefore imply that the practice could continue between churches within a diocese? Or does παροικία mean a parish, a congregation and the Canon therefore imply the total abolition of the practice?[11] However these questions are to be answered – and the scanty evidence precludes our answering them with any confidence – there is little doubt about the general tenor either of

Innocent's letter or of the fourteenth Canon. The early practice of expressing a wider sacramental unity through a sharing of the one loaf beyond the single congregation is in process of severe restriction. It may never have been very widespread, but motives of reverence for the elements seem to have ensured that any survival beyond the early centuries would have to be in a less strictly sacramental form, not using for this purpose bread that was actually a part of the consecrated eucharist.

In the last section we saw how the problem of the church's unity grew in complexity with the increasing size and number of Christian congregations and with the increasing mobility of Christians. In particular we looked at one sacramental means of expressing that wider unity, which can be traced in that early period but which was not destined to be a lasting or large-scale solution to the problem. And certainly the fourth century saw the problem growing very greatly and very rapidly in extent. With the increasingly favourable attitude of the Empire to the church congregations grew in number and Christians were able to travel more freely and more extensively. Moreover the Arian controversy in the early years of the century was a more world-wide phenomenon than any earlier comparable dispute within the church. Rival congregations were to be found in many centres, each out of communion with the other but each having a network of Christian groups in other places with whom they were in a state of mutual recognition and fellowship.

In such a situation a Christian was forced to choose where his allegiance lay. The barriers were seen as absolute barriers. To enter into communion fellowship with members of a congregation not in communion with your own implied cutting yourself off from your own fellowship. The second Canon of the Council of Antioch (AD 341) illustrates how seriously both any breach of communion fellowship and any fellowship with those out of communion were regarded. The Canon declares: 'All those who come to the Church of God and hear the sacred Scriptures, but do not join with the people in prayer or who in any irregular way (κατά τινα ἀταξίαν) turn away from the partaking of the eucharist shall be excommunicated until such time as they have done penance and shown by their deeds their change of mind, and can at their own urgent entreaty obtain pardon. And it is unlawful to associate with those who are excommunicated, or to assemble even in private houses for prayer with those who do not pray with the church, or to receive those who will not join with one church into another. If a bishop, presbyter, deacon or any other ecclesiastic is found to be associating with those who are excommunicate, he himself shall also be excommunicated as disturbing the order of the church.'[12] Two closely related convictions find expression in this canon. In the first place communion fellowship is so basic to church membership that any improper abstention from it leads to formal excommunication. And secondly communion fellowship is so profound a sharing with the whole body of the church that it must mean all that or it is a blasphemy. No kind of religious association – let alone communion fellowship – is permissible with one who is not himself in communion with the whole church body of which one is a member. One could not conceivably have true communion fellowship with two different people or two different groups of people who were consciously and deliberately out of communion with one another.

The way in which this problem was experienced in practice is well illustrated by the story of Apollinarius's expulsion from the church of Laodicea. Sozomen, who records the incident, sees it as the real cause of the Apollinarian heresy; it is very doubtful if it was as crucial in that respect as Sozomen makes out, but that does nothing to destroy the significance of the incident for our present purpose. While returning from exile to Alexandria, Athanasius passed through the city of Laodicea. He was unwilling to communicate with George, the bishop of Laodicea, who was a supporter of the Eusebian party. He did, however, enter into close relations with Apollinarius. For this Apollinarius was excommunicated by George; he had committed the crime of communicating with one who would not communicate with the church, of which he was a member, in the person of its bishop. Apollinarius, according to our records, was not himself unwilling to be in communion with George; indeed he did his utmost to persuade George to receive him back into communion, but George remained inexorable. It was this incident, in Sozomen's judgment, that was the really decisive cause of the Apollinarian schism.[13]

Thus there was no sanctioned intercommunion between

members of the rival Christian groups, which were characteristic of the schism in Antioch and similar centres in the fourth century. Holding the views that they did about each other's faith, there could not have been such intercommunion – if communion fellowship had any reality or substance about it. They did not regard one another as deviants from the true faith in some particular points of interpretation. They were rivals, each seeing the other as having abandoned the foundation of true faith, as having failed to maintain on the one hand the unity and transcendence of God and on the other the full divinity of Christ. Communion fellowship, coexisting with such an evaluation of each other's faith, was not possible.

We probably approach nearest to the kind of disunity between Christian denominations which we know today in certain phases of the Donatist schism. Even so it is not very near. They too saw one another as incompatible rivals in a way vastly different from the ecumenical attitudes of the present day. But there were times of comparatively peaceful coexistence. By the fifth century the schism had been in existence for three generations and men had never experienced Christianity in Africa without it. A Donatist husband and Catholic wife could admit that they worshipped the same God and that there was something wrong in the fact that they did not worship him together. There is a note of genuine ecumenical concern in the words of Augustine when he writes: 'Husbands and wives find unity in their marriage bed and disunity at the altar of Christ . . . slaves and masters divide the God they have in common, who himself took the form of a slave, that by his slavery he might make all men free.'[14] Here at least is a recognition of the problem, a feeling of the pain and the wrongfulness of division. But despite such measure of recognition as Augustine could ascribe to Donatist Christians – even to the extent of acknowledging the formal validity of their sacramental ministry – there could have been for him no question of intercommunion. Communion fellowship was expressive of the love and unity which belonged essentially to the body of Christ, and despite all the complexities and qualifications of Augustine's far-ranging thought, that body was for him coterminous with the one visible, catholic church.

It would be wrong to draw any conclusions for our contemporary situation from this historical sketch. As we said at the outset, our situation is vastly different. Our evaluation of the truly Christian status of those with whom we disagree even on major issues is wholly different from the attitude of early catholic Christians to those from whom they were separated on issues of doctrine or church order. But these reflections do seem to me to underline a fact which is obvious but too often overlooked. The eucharist is, among other things, a sacrament of *unity*; but it is only a *sacrament* of unity within a local setting. The unity of the church is more than a local issue but it is to its local expression that the unitary and unifying aspects of the eucharist are directly and primarily related. To put the main emphasis in considering issues of intercommunion on its appropriateness in the light of the situation of the local church is not to despise or to deny the wider nature of the church's unity; but it is to be true to the nature of the eucharist as a sacrament of unity.

Notes

Introduction

1. 'Looking into the Sun' and 'Jerusalem, Athens and Oxford', in *Working Papers in Doctrine*, SCM Press 1976, pp.148–179
2. John Hick (ed.), *The Myth of God Incarnate*, SCM Press 1977

PART I

1. The Role of a Critical Theology in the Church Today

1. W. N. Clarke, *Sixty Years with the Bible: A Record of Experience*, New York, 1909, cited in R. T. Handy, *Religion in the American Experience*, Columbia University Press 1972, p.123
2. R. E. Prothero, *Life and Letters of Dean Stanley*, 1893, Vol. 2, p.170
3. C. F. Evans, 'Unity and Pluriformity in the New Testament', in *Christian Believing*, SPCK 1976, p.50
4. *Doctrine in the Church of England*, SPCK 1938, pp.82–3
5. J. N. Figgis, *The Gospel and Human Needs*, Longmans 1912, p.xi

2. Christology in an Age of Historical Studies

1. Second Visitation Charge in the Diocese of Oxford, 1893; cited by G. W. H. Lampe, 'The Bible since the Rise of Critical Study' in *The Church's Use of the Bible*, ed. D. E. Nineham, SPCK 1963
2. See p.7 above
3. A. Schweitzer, *The Quest of the Historical Jesus*, A. & C. Black, 1911, third edition 1954, p.397
4. J. D. G. Dunn, *Unity and Diversity in the New Testament*, SCM Press 1977, pp.226–7
5. For the argument of this paragraph, see also J. Hick (ed.), *The Myth of God Incarnate*, SCM Press 1977, briefly in my 'Christianity without Incarnation?' pp.3–4 and more fully in Frances Young, 'Two Roots or a Tangled Mass?', pp.86–121
6. See W. Pannenberg, *Jesus – God and Man*, SCM Press 1968, pp.53–114
7. For a brief statement of my reasons, see my *What is Theology?*, Oxford University Press 1976, pp.105–6

8. The phrases in inverted commas are taken from A. D. Galloway, *Wolfhart Pannenberg*, Allen & Unwin 1973, pp.73–4 who gives a sympathetic account of the place of apocalyptic in Pannenberg's thought. See also G. G. O'Collins, 'The Christology of Wolfhart Pannenberg' in *Religious Studies*, 3, October 1967, pp.369–76

9. I have argued this more fully in the article already cited, 'Christianity without Incarnation?'

10. See my 'Myth in Theology' in J. Hick (ed.), *The Myth of God Incarnate*, pp.148–66

3. Christian Theology in an Age of Religious Studies

1. H. Kraemer, *The Christian Message in a non-Christian World*, Edinburgh House Press 1938

2. M. Schlink, 'Theology and Mission in Germany in Recent Years', *International Review of Missions* XXVII, July 1938, pp.465, 471. Cited by E. C. Dewick, *The Christian Attitude to Other Religions*, Cambridge University Press 1953, p. 41

3. See E. C. Dewick, op. cit., p.125

4. J. Maritain, *Redeeming the Time*, Geoffrey Bles 1943, pp.105f.

5. See p.8 above

6. Simone Weil, *Waiting on God*, Fontana 1959, pp.137–8

PART II

4. The Patristic Appeal to Tradition

1. J. L. Houlden, *A Commentary on the Johannine Epistles*, A. & C. Black 1973, p.53

2. Eusebius, *HE* iii, 39, 3–4

3. Polycarp, *Ep. Phil.* 3

4. Irenaeus, *Adv. Haer*. iii.1.1

5. Ibid., i.8.1

6. Ibid., iii.4.1

7. Ibid., iii.3.1

8. Tertullian, *De Corona* 2

9. Id., *De Virginibus Velandis* 1

10. Id., *De Corona* 3

11. On this issue I am much indebted to a paper by Hilary Armstrong entitled 'Pagan and Christian Traditionalism in The First Three Centuries AD' delivered at the Seventh International Conference on Patristic Studies in Oxford, September 1975. See also my remarks on 'respect for antiquity' in 'The Uses of "Holy Scripture" ' pp.74–6 below

12. For a fuller development of this theme, see 'The Role of a Critical Theology in the Church Today' pp.1–13 above

13. R. Hart, *Unfinished Man and the Imagination*, Seabury Press, New York, 1968, p.41

5. In What Sense is Christianity a 'Historical' Religion?

Originally published in *Theology*, LXXXI, January 1978, pp.4–14

1. C. H. Dodd, *History and the Gospel*, Hodder & Stoughton, revised edition 1964, p.21. Quoted by R. Page, 'C. H. Dodd's Use of History Critically Examined', in *Theology*, LXXIX, November 1976, p.329
2. J. H. Drury, *Tradition and Design in Luke's Gospel*, Darton, Longman & Todd 1976, p.1
3. G. D. Kaufman, *Systematic Theology: A Historicist Perspective*, Scribner, New York 1968, p.280
4. Cited by A. R. Vidler, 'Historical Objections', in D. M. MacKinnon, H. A. Williams, A. R. Vidler and J. S. Bezzant, *Objections to Christian Belief*, Constable 1963, p.58
5. M. Kähler, *The So-Called Historical Jesus and the Historic Biblical Christ*, Fortress Press 1964, p.118
6. J. M. Creed, *The Divinity of Christ*, Fontana 1964, p.106
7. Ibid., p.107
8. Ibid., p.106
9. A. G. Hebert, *Fundamentalism and the Church of God*, SCM Press 1957, p.43
10. Hebert regularly uses a capital P in this context.
11. David Cairns, 'The Motives and Scope of Historical Inquiry about Jesus', *Scottish Journal of Theology*, vol. 29, 1976, p.352
12. E. Brunner, *The Mediator*, Lutterworth 1934, pp.30 and 154
13. Ibid., pp.373–4
14. John Austin Baker, *The Foolishness of God*, Darton, Longman & Todd 1970, Fontana edition 1975, pp.276, 274, 277–8. See also my *The Remaking of Christian Doctrine*, SCM Press 1975, pp.77–8

PART III

6. The Holy Spirit in Christian Theology

Originally published in *Theology* LXVI, June 1963, pp.233–7

1. N. Berdyaev, *Spirit and Reality*, Geoffrey Bles 1946, p.22
2. Justin, *Apology* i.13
3. Athenagoras, *Supplicatio* 9
4. Origen, *Contra Celsum* 7.3
5. See 'Some Reflections on the Origins of the Doctrine of the Trinity' in my *Working Papers in Doctrine*, SCM Press 1976, pp.1–17

7. The Uses of 'Holy Scripture'

Originally published in Morna Hooker and Colin Hickling (eds.), *What about the New Testament? – Essays in Honour of Christopher Evans*, SCM Press 1974, pp.155–164

1. C. F. Evans, *Is 'Holy Scripture' Christian?*, SCM Press 1971.
2. Ibid., p.36.
3. Ibid., pp.29–30.
4. Basil Mitchell, *The Justification of Religious Belief*, Macmillan 1973, pp.155–6.
5. See Diogenes Laertius, *Vitae Philosophorum*, VIII 21.
6. Ps. 137.9.
7. W. Jaeger, *Paideia*, Vol. III, Berlin 1947, p.269; ET Blackwell 1945, pp.194–5.
8. A. D. Nock, *Conversion*, Oxford 1933, p.241.
9. S. G. F. Brandon, 'The Holy Book, the Holy Tradition and the Holy Ikon' in *Holy Book and Holy Tradition*, F. F. Bruce and E. G. Rupp (eds.), Manchester University Press 1968, p.15.
10. G. Widengren, 'Holy Book and Holy Tradition in Islam' in op. cit., p.219.
11. M. Iqbal, *The Reconstruction of Religious Thought in Islam*, Kashmiri Bazar, Lahore 1962, p.181.
12. T. F. Torrance, *Theology in Reconstruction*, SCM Press 1965, pp.21–2, 58, 87–8; *Theological Science*, Oxford University Press 1969, pp.22–3. Torrance himself gives to the distinction a far more comprehensive epistemological significance than I have in mind here, or indeed am able to accept.
13. Augustine, *Confessions* XII. xxiv–xxv.33–4.
14. H. I Marrou, *Histoire de l'éducation dans l'antiquité*, 6th edition, Paris 1965, p.246; ET, *A History of Education in Antiquity*, Sheed and Ward 1956, p.162.
15. Ibid., p.333 (ET p.224).
16. See W. Jaeger, op. cit., Vol. II, p.289 (ET p.214). Jaeger compares its authority with that of the Bible and the church fathers in the Christian era.
17. P. Brown, *Augustine of Hippo*, Faber & Faber 1967, pp.259–60

8. Eucharistic Theology – The Value of Diversity

Originally published in *Thinking about the Eucharist:* Papers by members of the Church of England Doctrine Commission, SCM Press 1972, pp.115–122

The paper was written at the end of the Commission's discussions and owes much to ideas and suggestions of other members of the

Commission. But they are in no way responsible for the way I have used those ideas and suggestions.

9. Sacramental Unity in the Early Church

Originally published in J. Kent and R. Murray (eds.), *Church Member-ship and Intercommunion*, Darton, Longman & Todd 1973, pp.35–49

1. Cf. J. Y. Campbell, 'The Origin and Meaning of the Christian Use of the Word "Ecclesia" ', *Journal of Theological Studies*, xlix, 1948, pp.138–40; reprinted in *Three New Testament Studies*, Brill 1965, pp.50–2
2. Cf. K. F. Nickle, *The Collection*, SCM Press 1966; O. Cullmann, *Catholics and Protestants*, Lutterworth 1960, pp.34–41
3. See G. La Piana, 'The Roman Church at the End of the Second Century', *Harvard Theological Review*, XVIII, 1925, pp.201–78; S. L. Greenslade, *Schism in the Early Church*, SCM Press 1953, pp.25–6, 99–101
4. Eusebius, *HE*, v,24,15
5. See L. Duchesne, *Liber Pontificalis*, 1886, 1.xxxiii (p.169, n.4) and 1.xl (p.216, n.2)
6. F. Lauchert (ed.), *Die Kanones der wichtigsten Altkirchlichen Con-cilien*, 1896, p.75
7. See G. W. H. Lampe, *Lexicon of Patristic Greek*, Oxford University Press 1961–68, p.570
8. PL, XX, 556–7
9. Lauchert (ed.), op. cit., p.72
10. As is generally assumed, e.g. Lampe, *Lexicon of Patristic Greek*, p.1042
11. The precise meaning of the term παροικία at this stage of its development is very difficult to determine. We have already seen in Innocent's letter an example of its use to mean 'parts of a diocese outside the main city' and there is an exact parallel in Basil, *Ep.* 240 (PG XXXII, 897B). P. de Labriolle examines the whole question in an article entitled 'Paroecia' in *Recherches de Science Religieuse*, XVIII, 1928, pp.60–72, and shows that even in official documents the words παροικία and διοίκησις are not used with precise and distinct meanings in the fourth century. It seems to me probable that the canon here under considera-tion is intended to restrict the practice of sending the sacrament to other churches more drastically than is generally assumed. The idea that the practice ever existed between different dioceses seems to depend chiefly on a misreading of Irenaeus's letter to Victor, which under-stands the practice there referred to, to involve a sending of the sacra-ment from Rome to churches in Asia.
12. Lauchert (ed.), op. cit., pp.43–4. The authenticity of the ascrip-tion of these canons to the Dedication Council of Antioch is doubtful; they may very probably belong in fact to a council much nearer to the

time of Nicaea. Cf. W. Telfer, 'Paul of Constantinople', *Harvard Theological Review*, XLIII, 1950, pp.55–6

13. Sozomen, *HE*, vi, 25
14. Augustine, *Ep.*, 33, 5

Index

Index